THINKING
FROM THE
INFINITE

If you do not change directions, you may end up where you are heading.

Lao Tse

THINKING
FROM THE
INFINITE

*Living Your Life
Outside the Box*

DR. CARELL ZAEHN

DeVorss Publications
Camarillo, California

THINKING FROM THE INFINITE

Dr. Carell Zaehn

Library of Congress Control Number: 2003113784

ISBN: 0875167969

First DeVorss Edition 2004

DeVorss & Company, Publisher
P.O. Box 1389
Camarillo CA 93011-1389
w w w . d e v o r s s . c o m

Printed in the United States of America

Contents

Dedication

It is with enormous gratitude to my teachers of metaphysics and true spirituality that this writing is offered. Its intention is to inspire and uplift others to be the best they can be, to make the most of the lives they've been given. The tools offered herein are the same tools offered to me twenty-five years ago. They are guaranteed, provable, repeatable—that is, they work every time. I offer to you what has been so generously given to me. May you take it, apply it and enjoy your life to the max.

Great thanks are due to Dr. Bill Little of the Pacific Coast Church of Religious Science in Pacific Grove, California, my spiritual mentor and life friend whom I value beyond words. Thank you to Cathy Cole, Kim Yalda, Steve Bergman, for their creative support, and to Dr. Rick Moss for helping clear the path.

Foreword

For the past 150 years the world has been the beneficiary of practical mysticism. Modern metaphysical giants such as Phineas Quimby, Mary Baker Eddy, Dr. Ernest Holmes, Emma Curtis Hopkins and many others have given clear insights into how to live the ancient teachings everyday.

Jesus said, "It is done unto you as you believe," but he did not give instructions on how to put this into action when we come up short at the end of the month. These illumined teachers and writers did just that. Ernest Holmes even created a powerful and simple method of prayer, called Treatment, that uses the ancient understanding in a scientific way to "return to the Father's house," where all that the Father has is ours.

Carell writes in this tradition of putting the scriptures into action. Her tone is funny and inspiring and yet she never leaves the wisdom of the ages. After reading this golden volume you will have tools to reshape your life mentally, emotionally and physically. She cuts through layers of philosophy and gets right down to it: How do you heal the cat? How do you accept increased income? This is a book for modern times and modern people that is based on timeless truth. Ernest Holmes would love this.

Enjoy your newfound freedom!

DR. BILL LITTLE

Introduction

In 1926, Ernest Shurtleff Holmes introduced a work entitled *The Science of Mind*. It was one of the masterworks of the New Thought Movement, whose turn-of-the-century mystics and poets had realized that everything is made up of God-stuff—Consciousness— and that if one were to tune into that way of looking at reality, some amazing experiences would occur. By aligning with universal order, wholeness and perfection, one could call those qualities into one's life.

Ernest Holmes' work expanded to create centers for learning the Science of Mind. Many of those centers have become known as Centers of Creative Living or Churches of Religious Science (not to be confused with Scientology). They all take Holmes' visionary experiences as a baseline in metaphysical thinking. None of it denies the Christian experience, or Judaism, or any of the major religions. In fact, it sees the thread in all of them because it recognizes the One Indivisible Truth that runs through them all.

One of Holmes' great gifts to all is the technique he called "Treatment." It came from the early years of the last century, when medical practice gave treatments to people in need of healing. Some of the early healers began to observe that doctors and assistants were able to heal their patients by recognizing the inherent divinity within the individual, and in doing so, jumped track for the patient and called forth the actual experience of wholeness in the form of instantaneous healing.

What is so amazing is that these early healings and the knowing of the real truth on behalf of a person were not odd in and of themselves. However, not very many people had access to this information back then and so this kind of thinking was considered unconventional.

At the millennium, this level of understanding is forefront. The techniques of treatment that were so amazing a century ago are now re-presented to you. They are still just as powerful—and available to you now.

This book takes the proven means of co-creation with the Higher Power and puts it into modern, practical application. Not only does it give you the tools and the wisdom, it "workshops" it for you step-by-step to give you the direction and support you need to do this process on your own.

Many self-help books give you ideas and philosophy, but are of no help in putting it all together. This book gives you the opportunity to write, practice, and play with your ideas with neither criticism nor "shoulds."

In the back of the book, you'll find resources of like-minded organizations, people and publications to assist you in unfolding your new knowledge.

Ernest Holmes always wanted his knowledge and teachings to be "open at the top." I know he would be really pleased by this presentation and its practical application of truth.

CARELL ZAEHN

THINKING
FROM THE
INFINITE

PART ONE

Don't wait for a major event
in your life to occur
before you begin to live.
Begin where you are.
Work where you are.
The hour you are wasting now,
dreaming of some far-off success,
is crowded with possibilities.
When you take the first step,
Your mind will mobilize
all its forces to assist you.
Once you have started,
All that is within and without you
will come to your assistance.

CHAPTER 1

THE SMILE
ON YOUR FACE

You've got to wake up every morning with a smile on your face
And show the world all the love in your heart.
Then people gonna treat you better.
You're gonna find, yes you will
That you're beautiful as you feel.

CAROLE KING, *"Beautiful"*

People who start their day with a smile are the ones who look for what they can bring to their day, not for what the day can bring to them. They are seeking to express themselves, their own special, unique identity. The glowing result of that self-expression is a natural giving back to the world. They can't help it. There's a magic about us when we're truly being ourselves, when we trust that our own uniqueness is not only enough, it's the best!

We all want to be happy, don't we? Don't you? Everybody would like to wake up happy in the morning. Some people do. They live joyous, contented lives. They are productive people, regardless of the arena of their expression. They are happy on the home front, at their jobs, with their friends and families. Life just seems to work for them. It seems the Universe has no problem answering their prayers.

Everyone has times when they don't feel empowered, are not having clarity on issues, and are missing the zing and enthusiasm for life's adventures. And some people just work around it. They don't get trapped in the outer issues, but maintain spirit and poise.

So how do the happy, successful, contented people find success in creating the lives that everyone would like to have ? We've all got that something special in us that wants to get out and get expressed. The question is how to do that.

The answer lies in what you are creating in your life. Most of us think of creative self-expression as an artistic manifestation. We associate self-expression with leisure activities or the realm of arts, crafts, and design in any number of fields. (If you're looking to stoke up your creativity in this realm, I invite you to explore Julia Cameron's books *The Artist's Way* and *The Vein of Gold*.)

Creative self-expression to shape your life comes from the deep place within, and also expresses in the outer world. Let's not limit our creativity to art, music, theatre and activities that some might relegate to the outer periphery of our lives. We can be creative with our own lives. It is more than a possibility that we can be the artists in our own lives. We can (and should) be the directors and producers of our life's unfolding.

Most of us rarely realize that we have a choice about how we think, what we believe. We may never have associated our beliefs with our conditions. And so we may have continued to live a "life of quiet desperation," believing this to be our destiny, and we were simply stuck with it. Well, we're not stuck with it. We always have the free will to choose our destiny.

All you need to do is look and see how your beliefs are driving your energy to produce your experiences. What are you doing with your energy? You are the one to determine how your personal energy is used. The Universe supplies you with infinite energy to be used any way you want. You can use it to improve your life or destroy it. You can expand it or contract it. You can use it for good or mess things up.

The challenge/opportunity is how to get the energy of your life moving in an area where you want it to go. How do you get money moving in your life? How do you get the relationship in (or out) of your experience? How do you get fear out of your head and peace in your heart? What's to be done about all of the stumbling blocks in life that prevent you from being able to schedule the ski weekend or the family conference? Why do you keep having the same old problems over and over? Why does it seem that some people's prayers are always getting answered and yours are not?

The answer is that those people know how to use the energy of the mind effectively to create what they want, to bring the experiences and results they envision into their lives. They do this with the mind, by energizing thoughts with feeling for the things and circumstances they want in life. They use their creative self-expression to focus on the goal, and are able to "see the end in the beginning." To get what you want in your life, you have to put the energy on the end result first. The corresponding result naturally follows. This book provides you with the tools to do that.

One way we can know that we are aligned with the Life Force that is God is that we feel more and more alive. Notice what gives you aliveness and what diminishes you, deadens and numbs you so that you only skim the surface of life. Begin to say yes to what quickens and energizes, to that which brings joy and gratitude.

MARY MANIN MORRISSEY

CHAPTER 2

THERE'S ONLY ONE

*There's a power in the Universe for good
and you can use it.*

DR. ERNEST HOLMES, *The Science of Mind*

Ernest Holmes was one of the early American metaphysicians who successfully tapped into the secrets of how to use the mind to co-create with the Universe, how to use thoughts constructively to get the results you want. Holmes went on to create a teaching called Religious Science or Science of Mind (not to be confused with L. Ron Hubbard's Scientology). Along with turn of the century mystics and poets such as Thoreau and Whitman, Holmes realized that the Universe responds to our thought, and if we use our thoughts in a directed manner, we can more effectively determine the results. He agreed with many of the world's great religions, including Hinduism, Judaism, Buddhism, and Islamic teachings, that there is only One: one God, one Source, One Power.

It really doesn't matter what we call this energy that beats the heart and breathes the body. We can call it Spirit, a divine Presence, Love, Nature, Goodness. Even if you don't have a spiritual connection in your life, there's some mysterious principle that beats the heart, breathes the body, creates life and moves our world. Whatever that stuff is, there's only one primordial version of it, one basic phenomenon. It's an energy in the Universe. It has its own laws, just like gravity and electricity, whether anyone taught us that or not, whether we've believed that or not, and regardless of how we feel about God. So this book will call that energy Spirit, God, Goddess, Universe, Life. It's all those things. Feel free to call it whatever makes you comfortable.

This universal principle works the same as the principle of electricity or gravity. Even if you don't believe in it, it still works and you can use it positively or negatively. You can use electricity to light up your world or end a life with it. Electricity really doesn't care, does it? It works just the same. Gravity works all the time too. It doesn't care whether you wear a parachute on your free-fall jump or not, but if you're aware of the principle of gravity, you'll wear the parachute. We don't expect rain to go up; we know it rains downward and so we align ourselves with the laws of the Universe and get our umbrellas over our heads, not on the ground.

In the same way, the Universe has certain laws of manifestation, and if we align ourselves with them, we can light up our lives here too. The converse, of course, is that if we are unaware of the principles of the Universe, we can very well cause ourselves a lot of hardship due to plain old ignorance. It's not that we're unintelligent, but lack of awareness doesn't excuse us. Laws are impersonal, so there's no excuse for ignorance of the laws. The laws of the Universe continue to work whether we're paying attention to them or not. So we can conclude that it would behoove us to find out what these laws are and learn how to use them well.

When we take the principles of universal law and use them, we access a power that many of us have never imagined possible. It is a well known fact that the human mind taps into a very small portion of its potential. Being able to harness the infinite powers of the Universe is going to increase the unused potential in your brain and in your life! You are going to learn how to tap into the source of the Infinite, ask for what you need and bring it into your life!

Up until now, you may have believed you were an average person or maybe even an insignificant person with no power to control your life, and that it would be sacrilege to think you were on a par with the Infinite. But if there is only One, one Power, one Presence, then I guess that means it's being everything, now doesn't it? Doesn't that include you? Did you think that that God, Love, Spirit was everywhere present but not in you? Did you think that Spirit stopped a foot in front of you and you were something else? Not possible if there's only One, everywhere present, now, through all time and space. If there's only One and It's being everything, everything includes YOU! That means your basic nature is made of God-stuff.

We're not used to thinking so highly of ourselves. Self-worth is one of our most difficult issues and so we wonder why God would want to be us anyway. Well, get used to it. You're made of God-stuff and the totality of the Divine lives and dwells in you, as you, for the purpose of revealing Itself through you. Now that will re-arrange your thinking, won't it?

What we want to do here is adjust our old thinking, and some of this is going to be about God and our beliefs relating to religion. There is no need to toss faith out the window. The intention is not to dishonor those religious institutions that did their best to instill a spiritual ethic within us. The underlying Truth of all religious teachings is ecstatically beautiful, teaching unconditional, divine love and seeing God in each other.

Over hundreds of years, however, many of the original teachings have been interpreted, mis-interpreted, and disseminated through the under-standings of individuals less enlightened than the original Teachers. Therefore, some of those teachings delivered in recent centuries were less than uplifting, expansive, or inspiring. Some of the teachings many of us received were depressing, even condemning, and taught us we were less than complete, less than whole or not good enough. God came off as being the Critic, a censorious entity expressing little love for our errors of under-standing.

Not only did some of those teachings make us feel "less than," but we lost our power line to the Universe. Many of us were taught that it wasn't possible to talk to God directly, that an intermediary was required. We couldn't talk to our Source, we lost our lifeline, and our prayers turned out to be pleadings for help. We were left powerless. Was that because somebody thought we weren't worthy? Or that God was over there, and we were over here, being poor pathetic people who needed a connector? Although those ways of believing had their roots centuries ago, most of us have believed that way up to the present moment. No wonder so many people feel out of control and powerless in the face of their daily life circumstances and needs. We'd lost our awareness of being able to ask for what we wanted and then expecting the request to be fulfilled.

If you choose to focus your attention on the strengths of others, on the virtues of others, on that part of others that strives for the highest, you run through your system the higher-frequency currents of appreciation, acceptance and love. Your energy and influence radiate instantaneously from soul to soul. You become an effective instrument of constructive change. If your intention is to align your personality with your soul, and if you focus your attention upon those perceptions that bring to you in each situation the highest-frequency currents of energy, you move toward authentic empowerment.

GARY ZUKAV, *Seat of the Soul*

CHAPTER 3

THE POWER
OF BELIEF

Be careful what you ask for. You might get it.

Anonymous

W hat we have been taught is important because those teachings have created our belief systems. We've collected our beliefs from parents and families, friends, school systems, churches, movies, song lyrics, television, commercials. All the "good" ones, such as family, church, even our friends, purported to plant "good" ideas in us. Their intention was the best they were capable of offering at the time. However, more than likely they, too, were less than enlightened, literally or figuratively. Let's face it. If a well-intentioned person delivers their message and it is influenced by that person's ego, you get a distorted presentation of the truth, regardless of whether it was a teaching in the Middle Ages or the twenty-first century.

Then there's the realm of TV and commercials. Now you *know* the media and corporate sponsors have no interest in whether their programming is good for you, whether their message supports your life or not. They want to make money, and hope you will help them by buying into their messages and buying their products.

Unless we've done some work on ourselves, most of what we believe about ourselves is someone else's statements or beliefs, combined with our interpretations of their behaviors and ego desires. Some of those statements were well-meaning. Some were not.

And then we had our basic institutions attempting to mold our thinking, for better or for worse – and a lot of it was for worse! Did you have one of those church moments when they tried to tell you that if you did a certain behavior that you'd go to Hell? That you were bad? That nice girls don't do that . . . that if you made a serious error, you were "inherently wicked"? Hey! A couple of unconscious errors does not a bad person make!

Even our well-meaning parents have done unconscious things to us. I was in Washington State in a restaurant, sitting near a couple with their hardly-yet-verbal well-behaved child. I overheard the father saying, "No. You can't have any. You're bad." What could possibly be bad about a one-year-old?! At that age, the infant is a reflection of the parent. It's not even capable of being socialized at age one and a half. Bad? I don't think so! These are the kinds of experiences we have as children that tell us we are unworthy and they stick with us until we wake up and are conscious.

We've all been dis-empowered, reduced in our self-expression and self-worth because someone else had an opinion, an opinion we bought into for whatever reason. Perhaps we were overpowered by a condemning person. Maybe we were so young we had no life awareness, no life experience to discriminate between a positive belief and a negative one. Even as an adult, we often lack the discrimination to choose wisely in our beliefs, mostly because we just kept on working with the old thoughts.

The beliefs we hold are running our lives. If we believe we are helpless, worthless people, we won't be manifesting love, money, or success in our lives. We just won't believe we can or that we're worth it. But if we believe we're intelligent, competent individuals, we will expect success in our lives. A belief that says "I'm unlovable" turns us away from the very love we want. We may think "I'll never have enough money (love, friends)," and consequently our belief plays out just that way. Up until now, we've probably believed there was nothing we could do about it. At the very least we've felt trapped, defeated, certainly limited by those thoughts.

Remember the phrase, "I'll belive it when I see it"? Wayne Dyer turned that phrase around and used it as a book title, *You'll See It When You Believe It*. In other words, "When I believe it in my vision, I'll see it in my life." Since what you see inside is what you get on the outside, and all your beliefs are creating what you have in your world, it's vital that you turn your beliefs around so that the vision you are projecting from within is what you want in your life. What you see is what you get!

In reality, it's not so important that we change our circumstances as it is to change our beliefs about them. Henry Miller said, "One's destination is never a place but rather a new way of looking at things." When we see our world through new glasses, through new beliefs and understanding, our world looks very different. We get a clearer view, a brighter picture, and a nicer experience. The surprise is that when we readjust our thinking and change the prescription of our inner glasses, the outer circumstances automatically change to match our new beliefs. Our experience is recreated by the Universe according to our beliefs.

You can see here that the magic of this process starts with what we believe. You can't afford to wait to believe it when you see it.

It becomes the primary mission here to take a look at what you truly believe, and make the necessary and beneficial changes. That covers all the kinds of beliefs you hold—about raising children, choosing foods in your diet, the kinds of relationships you keep attracting, the interplay of personalities on the job, the condition of the car . . . to the amount of money in your wallet.

Everything in our lives has some basic belief tacked on—everything. Wow! So ask yourself now when was the last time you took inner inventory and looked at what you believe about even one or two aspects of your life? What do you believe about money? What do you believe about your worthiness to receive love? What do you believe about your importance as an individual? What do you believe about your right to speak your truth? Where did these ideas come from? Who told you this? Is it *true*?

There are zillions of beliefs in our heads and psyches. It will take a long time to review them all, and over time, life will provide us with the opportunity to reassess them, one by one. Beliefs that make us feel less than worthy demand examination, and release. Those beliefs that are uplifting and positive merit expansion in our lives.

The following pages teach you how to replace negative thoughts with positive ones, and identify the mind with beliefs and thoughts that will out-picture in your life in a more abundant, happy and productive way. No matter who said what ignorant thing about you, or what you accepted as someone else's perception of you, this technique of *treatment* will clear it all and take you to new experiences of wholeness and happiness. Everyone is valuable and worthy, and deserves to live a life that reflects that. That includes you. You deserve a life that puts a smile on your face.

CHAPTER 4

THE STUFF
OF SPIRIT

Because [spirit] is infinite, or limitless, it is everywhere, and therefore it follows that the whole of spirit must be present at every point in space at the same moment. . . . All spirit is concentrated at any point in space that we may choose to fix our thought upon.

THOMAS TROWARD, *The Edinburgh Lectures*

Troward's words define this basic, underlying premise of the Universe. Spirit is everywhere, plain and simple. When you really get this, you've got it all. The entire Universe is made up of Consciousness, an energy that's alive, pulsating, and able to be converted from one form to another. It is a receptive energy field awaiting your attention, to give you back the form of whatever you are projecting upon it. Everything is created out of this one pulsating Consciousness at every moment.

That means there is only ONE Presence—Love, Life, God, Energy, whatever you want to call it. This One is everywhere present, at all times. It is all-knowing, infinitely intelligent. There isn't anything that's not made out of this God-stuff, whether it's animate or not.

Because this Consciousness is being all things, it's being *you* too, your mind, your thoughts, your energy, *and* your entire life experience. Is that not truly amazing?! The Universe is being YOU! If you only take in this one idea and let it reverberate throughout your being, you've already had a major shift in consciousness.

The consequences of this kind of understanding are profound, because the degree to which you use this principle and are careful which beliefs you put out to the field of infinite possibilities determines how affairs unfold in your life. The more time you spend expanding this awareness of only One Energy being everything—infinitely powerful, infinitely loving—and consider the vastness of this idea, the more juice you create to be used for transformation in your life.

It's a very interesting little exercise to make a list of all the qualities of God, Life, Source, or the One (whatever your definition of the cosmic energy is). We've been taught that God is love. God is forgiveness, God is life. Absolutely! Why stop there? If God/Goddess is everything (please use your favorite term for the universal One from here on), isn't the list going to be endless? If God is a power for good, and this writing takes that viewpoint, what qualities should be on the list?

Here are some qualities of the Divine you may like to consider, and then you can add others that occur to you. OK, here we go:

GOD IS:

cause	omnipotent	omnipresent	now
love	joy	peace	power
light	infinite	success	upliftment
silence	spontaneous	humor	intelligence
wisdom	honor	integrity	organization
honesty	willingness	surrender	transformation
energy	kindness	patience	tolerance
creativity	imagination	inventiveness	abundance
wealth	fascination	order	appropriateness
harmony	attention	stupendous	manifold
stewardship	truth	growth	compassion
adventure	giving	generosity	freedom
beauty	magnificence	visionary	efficient
rhythmic	softness	playful	flexible
strong	pure	disciplined	colorful
dexterity	balanced	whole	nurturing

exuberant	sexy	fun	bold
caring	voluminous	dynamic	secure
prosperous	self-expressive	self-accepting	frisky
dynamic	splendorific	fantabulous	sensitive
intuitive	forgiveness	perfection	supply
exuberance	mobility	grace	interest
communication	encouragement	faith	sacred
life	security	adjustment	enthusiasm
fearlessness	ease	selflessness	individuality
divine	poise	protection	happy
release	confidence	purposeful	acceptance
timeliness	fulfillment	responsive	non-violent
guidance	vitality	focus	application
immediate	expressive	perseverance	implicity
courage	release	understanding	gratitude
responsibility	trust	clarity	balance
inspiration	expectancy	delight	tenderness
healing	adventure	open	rest
renewal	space	ability	

(add yours)

_____

_____

_____

_____

And there are more, many more to fit into this list. You get a feel for the kinds of energies with which you can align yourself. But let's be careful of thinking that some of these qualities are holier than others. If God is being everything, that means EVERYTHING, including some aspects that you may react to. Any one of these qualities is worth contemplation, just to see what can be revealed, just to see where you might expand your mind a bit more.

All of these qualities exist within you. This is your identity! You are universal God-stuff. This is the prototype for every life form, and when we need to heal, we can call upon the prototype for life, for a human body, for relationships. It is this original "blueprint" that we call upon to re-form our wholeness.

> *Everything you need you already have. You are complete right now. You are a whole, total person, not an apprentice person on the way to someplace else. Your completeness must be understood by you and experienced in your thoughts as your own personal reality.*
>
> WAYNE DYER

These are the energies with which you'll want to align yourself. Putting these energies into motion brings better results than what your past thinking has created. When you focus on these qualities, you are projecting them into the universe, and that's what you're going to get in your life. That means there's no room for the negatives. If what you think is what you get, don't you want to be choosing ideas from the above list instead of the downers that the world tries to project into your consciousness? We'll want to get very familiar with that galaxy of higher qualities. Our job here is to uncover them, to reveal them, to bring them forth to produce results for you.

You might enjoy going to your local bookstore and purchasing the set of *Angel Cards*, a tiny little deck with one of these qualities on each card, so you can pull one each day and let that idea reveal to you what it has to say within you. It will help support the focus on positive ideas in your life.

So when you think of Life, Love, Source, God, Creator, you needn't confine yourself to some tiny, remote definition. Stretch your mind as far as you can conceive a truly vast, infinite, all-inclusive concept. Expand your definition of goodness and wholeness. Why? This is the definition of YOU! Did you realize you are that terrific? Better yet, did you realize that you are *infinite*?! This is who you are! This is what you're made of! If God/Universe *is all there is* and It's being everything, including you, then what's true of God is true of you. Yes! It's true of you. So now you can start thinking better of yourself. You can conceive of yourself in a higher way. As Ralph Waldo Emerson said, you can begin to "live your life with the license of a higher order of being."

What this now means is that you can take this awareness of the real Source of who you are, and apply it to your life's circumstances to transform them into a nicer, kinder, more rewarding experience. You are beginning to have a new definition of what God is and who you are. If God is all there is, and It's being you and being all those qualities, and it's being your life, that means you can choose those qualities for your next experience. Since the mind of the Universe and your mind are the same mind, you can choose from the infinity of divine qualities and apply them to your life. You could choose joy, freedom, love, prosperity, enthusiasm, and healing in your life. Why would you consciously choose defeat when you can now choose success? Or peace? Or enthusiasm?

You may have inadvertently chosen lesser qualities prior to this moment. No matter. You'll choose what you want from here on. Or you may not have "chosen" any qualities at all. Think about it: if you don't choose a higher quality, you're passively choosing to accept whatever the world gives you. Not choosing is still choosing! It's making a decision not to choose the qualities you really want. If you don't choose something good consciously, you're guaranteed to get potluck from the entire array of possibilities, including the negative ones. It's very important to continually choose the qualities we want in our life, because what you think and choose is what you get. So think good stuff!

There is One Infinite Life acting through Law, and this Law is mental; the Law of Mind in action. We are surrounded by an Infinite, Subconscious Impersonal, Neutral Plastic, Creative, Ever-Present, Thinking Stuff from which all things come, which, in its Original State, permeates and penetrates all things. By impressing our thought upon this Substance we can cause It to produce for us that which we think, to the limit of our ability to mentally embody the idea.

ERNEST HOLMES, *The Science of Mind*

CHAPTER 5

THE LAW OF MIND
And
WHY THIS WORKS

The question is 'How quickly can you get your mind to return to silence?' because in silence you are connected to the unified field.

DR. BILL LITTLE

Just like the laws of gravity and electricity, there is a phenomenon in the Universe that takes your vision, your belief and projects it into form. As it says in the Bible, "It is done unto you as you believe." Here's where we need to be really clear. Whatever your current belief is about yourself, about others, about your abilities or about God, you're going to continue to project that into the Infinite Consciousness and therefore out into the world.

I always liked that line, "What you see is what you get." That is exactly the way the Universe works. However you see yourself, whatever you think of yourself or perceive about your circumstances, that's going to be your reality. If you keep on putting out the same beliefs, how can you ever have a different reality? Input equals output. You can't plant an apple seed and get an orange tree. So let's be really clear that we need to be awake and aware: what we are planting at every moment is going to take root in the Universe, and manifest for us according to our belief.

The ideas we have believed deeply and the thoughts we dwell on at great length grow into big trees of consciousness. It's only natural that we have some good thoughts and some not-so-good thoughts. It's also a great gift of the Universe that not every dark thought we ever have actually plays out. However, the nasty ones we spend a lot of time repeating in our minds do have enough time and energy to create something substantial. One thought of resentment does not a tumor make, but years of resentment over an issue is a setup for dis-ease. So it's important that we take an honest look at what we believe, what our attitude is about this person, that situation, and what we think the outcome is going to be.

The purpose of this book is to inspire you to rethink those situations that are not working out well for you and to create a new and higher experience. This is where you get to choose something better and expect it to happen. And why would it happen? What is it that takes your thought and makes it so? Why is it that as you believe, so it is done unto you?

Everything in the Universe is made of energy. It cannot be created nor destroyed. We all remember that from high school science class. There is a law that the Universe responds to your belief and moves it from the *energy of thought* into the *energy of form*. What you *can* do with this energy is change its form. And that's what we can do every day with our minds.

Frequently we think specific thoughts such as, "John is a total pain in the neck." We can indulge in that kind of thinking and then wonder later why we're having a stiff, sore neck that's making life miserable. It's easy to think it's John who's the cause of the problem. However, the fact of it is that since thought is creative, our thought of John as a pain goes on to manifest as a corresponding physical pain in the body. We do this to ourselves, creating our own pain and misery. We stew and brew and run all this energy trying to deal with how we feel about John, getting a pain in the neck over it. We're only hurting ourselves.

We could be having better thoughts *and* a better day. We could take this kind of energy and change it into something higher, resulting in a better experience with John. The best result is that we're no longer irritated. We cease to be affected; because we're no longer invested in his behavior. We've pulled the emotional plug on it because we've released him to his highest good via the Law of Mind.

Is this the only situation in our lives where we do this? I don't think so!

What about money? Maybe you think you don't deserve to be prosperous. Maybe you don't believe you should be wealthy because mom and dad SAID it wasn't spiritual to have money. Hey, my mom said we weren't to talk about money and that translated into "money is secret," meaning it was something to be ashamed of. How about the priest who said it wasn't spiritual to have money or to like money? Worse than that, we'd go to hell over money. It's not the abundance that's not spiritual. It's being more attached to money than to Spirit that causes the problem.

Suppose we have the belief that it's not spiritual to have money, especially lots of it. We've taken someone else's understanding, such as it was, adopted it as our own, and are now living a life of lack when we could be having all we need and all we want. Unbeknownst to ourselves, we are causing our own suffering when a change of belief could create a different circumstance.

What about an abusive environment? No one would consciously sign up to be the victim in any form. On the outside, it looks like it's the tyrannical boss or the bully down the block who is doing all this to us. But are they doing these things to us, or have we been holding an incorrect view of our own value? If we hold a limiting view of who we are, the Universe has to fulfill it. It has to fulfill it because the thoughts and beliefs we hold and nourish play out in the world. As we change our view of ourselves and our circumstances, our experience changes automatically.

The Bible says "It is done unto you before ye shall have asked." That means that it is done unto you according to all those unexamined beliefs you've held for so long, the ones operating automatically at the subconscious level, that continue to play out automatically. Before you even get to think about what you believe, the Universe is already giving your beliefs back to you in the form of your experience.

The phenomenon of the Universe that takes what you believe and returns it to you is called The Law of Mind. It's just like electricity and gravity. Invisible, impervious to our beliefs, it's still working. You can't afford NOT to believe in gravity or electricity. That would have very dangerous consequences. It's also very dangerous to our souls and spirits to be unaware of the Law of Mind that manifests our beliefs into form. This Law is *impersonal* and totally amenable to suggestion. What you put into it, it gives you back in concrete experience. What you think is what you get, so choose the best and make it happen!

The really terrific thing about this impersonal law is, it really doesn't care who you are any more than electricity cares. It just works, and works every time, just like gravity and electricity. Thank goodness you don't have to be popular, or famous, or wealthy to be able to use electricity, gravity or this Law of Mind. You don't even have to make it work. That's what the laws of nature do; they work all by themselves. That is why you need to be alert about what you're giving it to work with. The Law really doesn't care who you are or whether you're just playing around. It's literal. It takes your word and makes it manifest. It's an energy that operates deductively, meaning it only operates from one point, one belief, one thought, the one thought that you give it to work from. It doesn't reason. It's an automatic "Give me the thought and I'll make it into form" phenomenon.

So when you start making your requests to the Universe, all you do is ask. But ask consciously! And the rest of the good news is that you're not the one responsible for making it happen. You get to have a mental vacation from worry and control, and that's a huge relief!

Your job is to choose wisely and with enthusiasm. Choose wisely because it's more productive than not. Choose the *best*! Why would you want anything less than the best? Choose enthusiastically because you get better results. Why? Take a look at the word *enthusiasm*. It comes from the Greek, meaning *to be with God*. So when you get enthusiastic, you've got divine power and support behind you. There's an old time metaphysical phrase that says, "In the feeling is the healing." Get your excitement going for this thing you are requesting of the Universe and you'll get bigger results a lot quicker.

As spiritual beings having a human experience, we lift our perspective through prayer. When we pray, we align our thinking with God's thought. As Emmet Fox wrote: "Scientific Prayer will enable you, sooner or later, to get yourself, or anyone else, out of any difficulty on the face of the earth. It is the Golden Key to harmony and happiness." Simply try it for yourself and see.

MARY MANIN MORRISSEY

CHAPTER 6

THE HOW OF TREATMENT

Putting it into Practice

We come into the absolute exactly in proportion as we withdraw ourselves from the relative; they vary inversely to each other.

THOMAS TROWARD, *The Edinburgh Lectures*

To manifest something new in your life, you need to change the pattern or belief you are currently using. There is a specific sequence in using the mind to make those changes most efficiently. This is called *treatment*. Here is the basic format of doing a treatment/prayer for the purpose of manifesting and creating:

STEP ONE:	RECOGNITION
STEP TWO:	UNIFICATION
STEP THREE:	SPECIFICATION
STEP FOUR:	RELEASE AND GRATITUDE

It's Spirit first, add "you" second, re-view the problem third, then let go and say thanks. That's the nutshell version. We'll take a look at each step, spend a little time with each of these areas to get your power packed into it, and then see how it all goes together. Then when you do your treatment, it's got impact.

Before we continue, here is a treatment for you, the reader. This will give you the experience of what this process does and how it flows. Close your eyes for a few seconds to get into that quiet, inner space. Take a couple of deep breaths. Then open your eyes and read this to yourself, preferably aloud.

TREATMENT:

This treatment is for me. The truth is that there is only one Divine Intelligence, one Source of Knowledge, one Energy in the Universe. It is whole, complete, permeating all space and time and it's being me right now. This Divine Knowing knows exactly how to use this information perfectly. There is only One Universal Mind. One, not two or twenty or ten million. This One Mind is my mind now and it communicates this information to me and through me easily and effortlessly. The light of understanding is on. The Ah Ha! Experience is at hand.

Not only do I choose to understand this technique, I choose to be able to use it effectively. Any thoughts that this was going to be a complicated process, or that I would not get it are now eliminated as Infinite Intelligence illumines my mind fully and with grace. The joy of having this treatment process available for my upliftment and unfoldment delights my mind and my soul. All my statements are easy and effortless as Spirit takes these truths and blesses my life with them. My world now radiates in the light of positive thinking and good choices and the fruits of the treatment illumine and grace my life. Divine Wisdom and Intelligence are now flowing fully and completely as my mind now.

I release this treatment to the Law of Mind. I am not responsible for manifesting this truth. It's not my job. The universal law takes this declaration and carries it out to the letter. The Law of Mind has received this information and is now busy rearranging my mind, my perception and my understanding. So I let go and am thrilled that I already got it, that I got the understanding and can now use it for myself and for the good of others.

Thank you, Spirit/God/Goddess for this wonderful experience. It's great! I'm so pleased. And so it is!

STEP ONE
Recognition
"Yea Spirit"

If you find yourself in a hole, the first thing to do is stop diggin'.

WILL ROGERS

The first step of treatment is the realization that the problem is not going to be of any help at all in fixing things. Remember, you can't solve the problem from the level of the problem! Step One is that sudden Ah Ha! when you realize that you could be talking to the Universe instead of continuing to struggle with the situation. This is the moment of the paradigm shift, shifting from the circumstance to talking to the Universe. You just simply withdraw your attention from the issue, and go inside yourself and remember that there's only ONE. Stop dwelling on the challenge and put your attention on the Source, the One, the Infinite Field of Primary Cause. This is where you get in touch with that energy that beats your heart and breathes your breath. It's the primordial energy of the Universe, the ultimate Creator of all. That's where you start. That is where you make your connection to the power to make changes.

Take your mind back to a recent problem, a drama in your life. Think back on how you tried to fix it. The likelihood is that you kept working and reworking it, thinking about the problem and not finding a way out. A solution was difficult to come by. That's because we try to make the problem into the solution too.

The reason we have so much difficulty in solving life's problems is that we consider the issue from the same level as the problem. It's the ego that thinks that if it can control just this one thing, just one more time, we can fix it ourselves. The problem is the problem; it is not the solution. Think about it. How can the problem be the solution? Of course it can't. That's why you get on the phone and call someone to discuss the issue with, to see what new ideas they have to offer. You're looking for a new perspective because your old one obviously isn't working. You're looking for clarity, solution, resolution, and you're never going to get that from the problem, that's for sure. Maybe your friend will offer something helpful. (Let's hope your friend is in a state of detached upliftment and clarity when you call.)

But why limit yourself to one person's opinion, even if it is better than yours? You could be accessing the entire Universe!! If the Universe is being you and your mind, why not pick a solution from the vast array of infinite choices? Up the ante. You've got all kinds of solutions at the fingertips of your mind. Why limit yourself to one solution when you can have lots of choices? Tap into them all!

What happens when you do this is you instantaneously *jump track* and enter an expanded reality. Now you have choices of solutions from the vast reservoir of universal energy. Now you're calling up all the power of the entire Universe so you can use it to break through limiting beliefs and transform your experience.

Spend enough time in Step One identifying those qualities of Universal Spirit that you'd rather be part of. Get into that list of qualities on paeg 14 and find some that are true of your new experience. Say to yourself, "There is only ONE. One power, one presence, one life. It is whole, complete. It is perfect. It is infinite intelligence and therefore knows exactly the perfect solution to this drama," or something akin to that. Make the Divine qualities yours, and know that they are what Spirit is being in your life now.

This is a good time for you to make some statements about Spirit, Life and Universe. Write as many statements about Spirit/God/Universe as you can come up with. Write at least two lines that you think are true of the Universe all the time, such as "There is only One Divine Intelligence" or "The only creative power is pure Consciousness." Then write a few lines that are more specific, such as "Spirit is infinitely imaginative" or "God is abundant energy," something you might use to address a specific circumstance. We're not going for fancy here.

Anything you write that embodies the Universe as the One, Only and First, is perfect.

PRACTICE TIME: RECOGNITION

_____

_____

_____

_____

_____

_____

_____

_____

_____

_____

_____

_____

_____

_____

_____

_____

_____

_____

_____

_____

_____

_____

_____

_____

_____

_____

_____

_____

_____

_____

_____

_____

_____

_____

_____

_____

_____

_____

The more time you spend here, reminding yourself that God/Goddess/Spirit is always being these qualities and is being them right NOW, the more powerful (and instantaneous) your solution is going to be. So linger here, impressing yourself with the magnitude of universal power and the benevolence of Spirit.

This is the part I call *Yea Spirit!* because it's extremely energy-generating to get all jazzed up about how terrific God/ Spirit is. The Universe's good qualities are so much more appealing than what the issue is. So here's to *Yea Spirit!* and feel free to make it into *Yea Goddess!* or *Yea Life!* or *Yea Peace!*—whatever fries your shorts and puts a smile on your face.

You are preparing to replace an old belief, so remind yourself of these higher energies of God/Goddess that are available and happening in this moment. If you've always thought your God was a punishing God, here is the moment to declare that God is all loving, supporting, nurturing, caring for all your needs.

Now you get to claim that God/Life/Universe is the balm of healing to your soul, that It transforms all your old beliefs and lifts you up in Spirit. That part sounds a little "churchy," right? It just may seem a little more logical now. This is the time when you take everything you wished God/Life was for you and choose it. Make it real. Make it BIG! FEEL it! Breathe it. Expand it! Get excited about it! No need to be in a hurry here. You can bliss yourself out just contemplating the magnificence of divinity in this instant.

When you go deep within in meditation and reach the place where there is perfect silence and absolute stillness, you've touched the place before thought. Because you are in the realm of the not-yet-thought-of, not-yet-spoken, and not-yet-heard, *you are free to create any thought here and send it out into time and space*. That's why this is so powerful. This place of silence is the place of pure being, pure consciousness, not being this or that. It's your being and the beingness of everything in the cosmos. This the place of creation.

Therefore, the more you allow yourself to rest and breathe in this space of silence, the deeper you are in contact with the totality of the

Universe, with Source. When you choose an experience from this place, you are directing the entire Universe, and it has to respond because the Law of Mind is going to take you at your word, literally, and reproduce the thought as experience in the outer world. You have the whole of creation at your disposal.

Therefore, to prepare to do an affirmative prayer treatment, take a moment to become still within. Take a few slow, deep breaths and contact that deep stillness. When you feel prompted, make your declarations of the truth of the Universe (Step One). They will be much more powerful because the more contact you have with the inner stillness, the more power you have to energize the words you will be speaking or writing.

It is essential for you to operate in present time. We only have the present moment to work with. As we declare our choices about what we want to the Universe, we want it to happen now. The real truth is that there is no past and no future. The past is only an historical memory. The future is not here either; it doesn't exist yet.

You're going to create out of the present moment, so you want to be sure you handle the now very well, with conscious attention and good intent. You want your healing now, don't you? Of course you do! When you feel that deep, inner quiet, the Source, it's *now*. Yes, it may be true later, too, but we're not doing later. We're doing *now*. You don't want your solution later. You want it now. And the fact is *Spirit is now*, in the present, everywhere present at any moment, all powerful, omniscient, and it's all happening right here, right now. Do not put your good off until later. With every choice, be sure you declare it for now, i.e. "God is protection NOW. God is resolution NOW. Spirit is love NOW, Consciousness expands me NOW."

Simply do this:

Be still, and lay aside all thoughts
Of what you have learned about the world,
All images you hold about yourself.
Empty your mind of everything
It thinks is either true or false,
Or good or bad,
Of every thought it judges worthy,
And all ideas of which it is ashamed.
Hold onto nothing.
Do not bring with you one thought
The past has taught, nor one belief
You ever learned before from anything.
Forget this world,
Forget this course,
And come with wholly empty hands unto your God.

THE COURSE IN MIRACLES

Most of us have lived our lives in the past or the future. We've either spent so much time rehashing all the old things that have happened to us long ago, or live in a fantasy of what we hope will happen in the future, that we miss the present moment altogether. You're not interested in repeating the past. Look where it *didn't* get you! And you can't get to the future without launching from the present, so BE HERE NOW! (Thank you, Ram Dass!) Do your spiritual work in the NOW, in the present. The future is created out of the now moment, so if you take care of the now, your future is guaranteed just the way you've chosen it.

We have habits of saying things like "*When* I'm well," or "My wealth *will* be manifest *soon*," or "My good *will* be coming." It's so easy to let these little words of "later" slip into our speech, i.e. "is going," "will be," "soon," "when," or even "if." They are words that prevent us from receiving our good, because if you declare your good for later, that's when you're going to get it. The solution will be later, if ever, not now when you need and want it. Stay vigilant that you don't let phrases of postponement creep into your declaration. The only moment is now. The past is gone, and you're creating your future out of this moment of choice, so be clear about working in the NOW. There is no time in pure consciousness!

Your present situation doesn't determine where you can go.
It merely determines where you're starting from.

©2002 MotivationMentor@aol.com

STEP TWO
Unification
"It's being me too!"

Treatment is not for the purpose of making things happen; it is to provide, within ourselves, an avenue through which they may happen.

ERNEST HOLMES, *The Science of Mind*

A common error in our thinking is believing that God/Life is indeed being all—but not me. That Spirit is everything—except for me. We may even believe that Life/Power/Goodness/Godness/ Goddess stops a foot in front of us. Isn't it interesting we can look at good all around us and think it's not being us too?! That's the old lack-of-self-worth syndrome held by many people. The Great Beings say that when we get to the edge of enlightenment, the last ego stronghold to go is our sense of unworthiness, wondering why God would want to be me anyway? So don't think less of yourself because it didn't occur to you that God was being you. Not only is God being you, It's being you at every moment, right NOW, full tilt, every cell, every organ, every person in your life, every thought you think. It's all of you!

It's very important to consciously unify with the Divine at this point because we have a tendency to think *Yea Spirit* and forget that we're part of the deal, that Life is really *Yea Life as Me*. Yes, God/Spirit is all there is, everywhere present, all powerful, infinitely compassionate, but the point is that because there's ONLY ONE, one Mind, one universal consciousness, that one Mind/Life is also being me NOW.

This is the point of remembering "it's me too!" If you don't line yourself up with Spirit, as Spirit, how is Spirit going to do the work *through you*? The only way life ever changes is when we let the Universe work through us, instead of at us. When we get aligned with Spirit/Life as us, all the power of the cosmos flows through our being, and then we get to release it all out into our world.

Most of us have never stopped to think that the entire Universe could flow through us, that we could be, and are, a channel of the Divine for expression in the world. The ego thinks it's here for its own gratification. It wants to tell us it is going to do everything and fix things, and we can sit back and let our ego minds take care of everything. Well, we've tried that now and it's not getting us to where we'd really like to be, now is it?

So instead of being a conduit for your self-invested ego, shift gears and become a conduit for the cosmos. Open up your energy circuits and invite Spirit to use you for good. See what happens. The likelihood is that after reading this passage you will not be an instantly fully God-realized cosmic being (but you might!). You can figure you'll have some practice time to get the hang of this new way of perceiving how you fit into the scheme of things and how important your personal role is in the unfolding of your life and the manifestation of your dreams. That's just fine. The Universe is unfolding you at the perfect rate, in perfect order.

This is the zone where you can state that all the aspects of universal greatness are being you now. You can say, "Divine Intelligence is being me now," or "All of the patience of God is being me now," or perhaps "God's light and harmony fill my being now." Whatever quality it is that you wish you had in your life, declare it as being you now. The buck stops here. No more thinking your good is over there somewhere. It's your job to declare that it's being true in you, right here, right now.

Enjoy what this feels like! This is pretty zingy stuff, if you ask me. Is this not seriously empowering?! For all of you who have had a propensity to give your power away and then wonder why your life isn't working, get into this! This is where you take your power back and get in cosmic charge! DON'T MISS THIS PART. Rise up and declare this truth to be yours! We don't want to give our good away because we think we don't deserve it. Everyone is entitled to their highest good. Are you going to reach out and take yours? YES, YOU ARE! You can go back to the practice lines and write, "I accept the truth that the loving, compassionate Universe and I are one. What is true of the Universe is true of me. I am a hologram of the totality, whole and complete in every detail. As an individualization of God, everything that is true of God is true of me (and everyone else as well)."

PRACTICE TIME: UNIFICATION

Write statements and phrases to state that you and the whole of the universal Power and Truth are one:

_____

_____

_____

_____

_____

_____

_____

_____

_____

_____

_____

_____

We need to be specific about our desires. We need to develop a clear, concise picture of what we want our lives to look like. Only then can that dream life manifest itself into physical form.

Say you and your best friend are standing in the kitchen. You say, "Hand me the metal object." They look around and see a spatula, a fork, a butter knife, a spoon, a pizza cutter. They are confused because they see all of these metal objects, but they don't know which one you meant. So they hand you a spoon. "That's not what I want," you say. They hand you a spatula. "That's not it either," you say. They would have to keep handing you everything in the kitchen until they got it right. On the other hand, if you had said, "Hand me a fork," you would have gotten it immediately.

Developing clarity about what we want is fundamental to our success. You see, the Universe wants us to have everything we want. The Universe is not manipulative or cruel. It is simply waiting for you to get crystal clear about what it is that you want.

MARK VICTOR HANSEN

STEP THREE
Specification
"So What?"

Evil (ignorance) is like a shadow that has no real substance of its own; it is simply a lack of light. You cannot cause a shadow to disappear by trying to fight it, stomp on it, by railing against it, or any other form of emotional or physical assistance. In order to cause a shadow to disappear, you must shine light on it.

SHAKTI GAWAIN

Now is the time to take all this truth and apply it to your life. You take the truth of what God/Spirit is and apply it to your situation. Weave God and Truth through your thoughts on the issue. Prayer is not about stooping to the level of the problem. It's about lifting the issue up to a higher level of consciousness.

This is the "yea" and "nay" department. Here is where you declare *exactly* what you want and what you don't want anymore. It's "Yes, I choose this experience now, and I no longer dwell in this negative idea." Perhaps it's "The Universe has got my issue totally in hand, *and* I no longer need or choose to worry about the unfoldment of the answer to the problem." Make some *positive* statements at this point to wipe out the facts of the problem with the truth of which you've just convinced yourself in Step One. You might find yourself saying:

"My cat is now healed, perfect and whole. I see divine perfection in every cell of its body, renewing its entire digestive system."

Or, "I give up my concern about being late for this interview and get on God's time. Perfect Intelligence knows exactly how to get me to my destination safely and at the perfect moment. On God's time, all affairs are in perfect order."

"There is no fear in divine consciousness. Life is love, peace, serenity and perfection, and unwavering calm. I now choose the instantaneous experience of absolute calm. My mind is focused and it is fearless."

"The One Mind knows exactly how to come up with the perfect new house for me in the right place, for the right amount of money, in a great neighborhood, with an ocean view, and finds it by August 11 of this year."

If the need is for the perfect wedding dress by Christmas, be specific about it because the Law of Mind is going to take you at your word and give you just what you asked for. Saying "I want something hot to wear" may well get you new shorts and a T shirt. You've got to be specific, such as, "I want a white wedding dress, strapless, with lots of lace, and a feeling that's traditional with an updated flavor." If what you need is a vacation and you've got your heart set on Fiji, say so! Declare something like, "I choose a 3-week vacation in Fiji with my wife, sailing and snorkeling. The accommodations are the best at the Grand Fiji Hotel and the view is terrific."

It's very important to be specific so the Universe can give you what you really want. On the other hand, it's not necessary to delineate so much that you make this hard for yourself—and for the Universe to deliver. For example, if you're looking for a new house, it's important to pick the community, this neighborhood or that one, nice neighbors, play area for kids, safety for the pets and maybe you need a granny unit for the in-laws. You don't want to go so far as to say that one bedroom is 9 x 13, the other two are 10x 15, bathrooms are painted ecru with Italian tile flooring, the kitchen has a brand R garbage disposal, and the house is painted Quaker blue with cream trim by Sherwin Williams. Well, it can certainly happen, but you might find it quicker to accept the workable basic necessities and create the rest in due time.

The point is that you don't want to delineate so much that Spirit has no room for what It has in mind that would most likely be even better than what you had in mind. After all, if Universal Mind is being your mind, doesn't it already know exactly what and where you need this great house? Be sure to give God some breathing/creating room for it to do what it does best. Your job is to choose. God's job is to pull it off. Please don't try to do God's job. Infinite Intelligence doesn't need help or control from you, just your attention and your desire.

Dwell not on the past. Use it to illustrate a point, then leave it behind. Nothing really matters except what you do now in this instant of time. From this moment onwards you can be an entirely different person, filled with love and understanding, ready with an outstretched hand, uplifted and positive in every thought and deed.

EILEEN CADDY

This is also an appropriate time to declare what is no longer true in light of all the truth you've declared in the beginning. You might say:

"There is no longer any room for fear in my consciousness."

"All my doubts are eliminated."

"There is no lack. My past money history has nothing to do with this moment."

"Any old beliefs that don't support my new money consciousness are now deleted, gone, finished."

"I no longer have time to fool around with worrisome thinking."

"All persons trying to hold up this transaction are now redirected to other interests. There's no blockage to this deal going through."

What you are doing in the "No" department is simply withdrawing your attention from that which you no longer want in your life. You state that you are removing your attention/belief from the undesired circumstance and placing it on the desired outcome. This is a key principle to manifesting your desires.

Keep working through as many Yes's to higher consciousness and No's to old ideas as you need to get clarity and resolution in your mind. There is *no* room for any negative thinking here. Insist on the positive choice, no matter how doubtful your mind is or how scared your ego, no matter the appearance of external circumstances. You *must* hold the vision of your goal until it manifests, so stay with the focus and clarity.

We're not interested in whether your friends or relatives agree with what you think or whether they are clear in their thinking. This work is going on in *your* mind, so you are the only one we are interested in at this point. Even if you are praying for your family member who is ill, it's your own thinking about it that has to be cleared up first. Take care of your thinking first and the rest will follow perfectly. It only takes one person to know the truth to change the entire course of events for eternity.

PRACTICE TIME: SPECIFICATION

Let's take a hypothetical situation for practice. Let's assume our buddy "Jeff" is interviewing for a new job tomorrow. Write several lines about what is true and what is not about Jeff 's opportunity.

Did you remember that he's got his new job now, that his good is not dependent on all the circumstances you see on the outside?

Intuition and Imagination

While you are speaking your Yes's and No's about what is true and what is not, there are two energies to invite into your treatments. They are intuition and imagination. They are both gifts from the Universe to assist you in your inner work.

Intuition is spontaneous, giving you sudden insights and wisdom about what's really going on with the situation. It may jump out at you. It may give you a wee inkling and whisper something like, "She's not really as nasty person. She's having so much pain because her child is out of control. She's fighting, not with me, but to hang on to her life." Then you can redirect your treatment from there, knowing peace, harmony, and life's unfoldment for her highest good and the highest good of all. The temptation may be to try to treat her into being a nicer person. But let's be clear that our job here is to know the highest for everyone, not to get them to be someone or some way our egos think they should be because we'd like it better that way.

The gift of intuition is the insight you need, that your worldly rational mind can't pick up. Intuition is God's mind flowing through you, so that you get the real facts, the real Truth. When that occurs, you shift your treatment to address what you've just been told from the inside. Take what God says about the situation and then declare it to the outside experience. Ask what God says about the situation and then speak it out. That's treatment from the highest point of view.

The other energy is imagination. We have this marvelous fertile imagination which we've used for daydreaming, fantasizing, and play. If you harness those positive visions and give them to the Law of Mind, they will become your experience in time and space. The Law of Mind holds your thought in infinite potential; it's got the power to form anything you can envision, so envision the end result right now, just the way you want it. Use your imagination to see the end in the beginning. See the results you want as being so now. Here's a good example:

It was Nelly Wright's first ever Big Sur International Marathon in 1988. She won! She won because she had envisioned herself winning the race beforehand. She told *The Monterey County Herald*, "I saw myself crossing the finish line in first place. I saw it all so clearly, and it all seemed very real— not like a dream at all. It was like it was really happening. Then I heard a knock on my door and I woke up. I actually had to wipe tears off my cheeks before I answered the door."

Now *that's* seeing the end in the beginning, seeing the desire as already fulfilled. Not only did Nelly see it, she *felt* it. So even if it feels like you're messing with your mind to think this way, remember that you are creating a new medium from which to birth your vision. Just let your imagination loose and get into it. See it. Smell it. Feel it. Get into it, just like Nelly. See it as already finished.

In the local newspaper I saw a photo journal article of a couple who had adopted a little Chinese girl. While they were waiting for the papers to be approved, they acquired five large paintings, each depicting a young Chinese girl. After the arrival of the new child into the family, they said they were surprised that the adopted child looked just like the girl in the painting. Is it surprising when one knows that the Law of Mind took their vision and executed it to the letter?

Not only should you see it as so in your mind, you should *act as if* it is already so as well. See yourself as the winner. Dress the part of the new executive. Act like you believe everything you've just set in motion.

Acting as though your vision is already a reality is very powerful. It continues to reinforce your treatment after you've done it and re-impresses your subconscious mind that you mean what you said. If you want to get a promotion, start acting like you already have it. You don't have to be an egopottamus about it. Just act in the new, competent, confident way. Someone will notice, especially Spirit, which will be automatic in realigning your outer world to match your new inner beliefs. Your desire will manifest so much faster and more perfectly because the Law of Mind will know you absolutely mean it. You direct the mind in treatment to tap into the flow. You use the imagination to show how you would like it formed in time and space.

A word of wisdom is appropriate here about "acting-as-if." Use some common sense. If you buy a lottery ticket and the lottery is worth two million dollars, it is not recommended that you go writing checks for the two million before you've been told you've won, just because you are seeing yourself winning. Let's at least make sure your faith and belief are equal to your enthusiasm. But if you've put in your cosmic request for a new job as executive director of a top corporation, you could start wearing the suits and looking the part. It places you in the *feeling* of it and empowers your vision.

Feeling is an important part of your manifestation. There's an old metaphysical expression that says, "In the feeling is the healing." What that means is that the prayer with the passion, the gusto, is going to create better results than an emotionally flat, mechanical statement. Remember that word enthusiasm, meaning to be with God? When you get enthusiastic, you've got zing going and the Universe takes it and says "Wow! That person really means business. She's not fooling around here. We better get going on this one!" So feel free to get jazzed up about your words. Shout them out! Get excited! Get some juicy energy flowing on it and enjoy the results!

> *To grow, you must be willing to let your present and future be totally unlike your past. Your history is not your destiny.*
>
> ALAN COHEN

STEP FOUR

Release and Gratitude

"Let Go and Let God"

Emerson said, "Prayer is the contemplation of the facts of life from the highest point of view." In learning how to pray, we practice letting go of our attachment to the outcome we have imagined and trust God to have the highest point of view.

MARY MANIN MORRISSEY

Dr. Raymond Charles Barker, former minister of the New York Church of Religious Science, used to tell about a delightful African-American woman in the South who was fantastic at instant releasing. Folks would come up to her on her porch and lament their miseries. She'd just rock back and forth, back and forth, saying, "T'ain't so. T'ain't so." She'd already denied the appearance of the problem and relaxed into that truth that the Universe was already at work revealing their wholeness. She was operating with a great sense of detachment about everything.

The Law of Mind is now taking your request and executing it to the last detail. The end is already guaranteed. Therefore, you don't need to fret and sweat about how the cosmic plan is going to pull this off. You don't have to worry about all the in-between steps of manifestation. The Law of Mind is quite busy arranging for your request, and it's probably coming up with a solution that's far more inventive and successful than what your mind was cooking up.

At the risk of embarrassing your ego, you have to admit that if your mind was so successful at solving this one, you'd already have the solution, right? So since you don't, it's a good indication that God's got a better idea for your highest good, and it's high time you got out of the way and let the Universe give you what you really need and want.

It is very important that you fully release this action to the Universe to take care of. You've got to get your fear, ego, and attachment to outcome out of the way. If you are either insistent on how it's going to turn out or worried about how it's progressing, you're not going to get the results you want. You will be destroying your sand castle. There's no sense building a vision on one side and simultaneously tearing it down on the other. So just get out of the way and let Spirit do what It knows best. Remember that God knows exactly what you need for your highest good and is giving it to you now. When your demonstration arrives, don't slam the door on it because you were expecting something else instead of resting happily in expectancy for your highest good.

> *It seems to me that we often, almost sulkily, reject the good that God offers us because, at the moment, we expected some other good.*
>
> C.S. LEWIS

The Universe is working perfectly for the highest good of all, right NOW, and so your problem is no longer a problem at this point. Given your newly revised understanding, you're free to trust the Law of Mind to take your new declarations and implement them. It's not your responsibility to make the Law of Mind work. That would be like trying to get gravity to work. It doesn't need your help, thank you very much.

There's no need to keep thinking about when your manifestation is going to materialize and what it's going to look like. Just detach from the belief that you have do be the do-er, the one to make things happen. Remember the Biblical phrase, "I of myself can do nothing. It is the Father within that doeth the work." It would be a detriment to your success to keep ruminating over the how's and why's of it when the Universe has got everything perfectly under control. (Ooooh! I know your ego hates that one!)

Now you're free, literally. You're free to just drop the whole thing because you're releasing it to the Law of Mind for manifestation. You've made your choice. Now you can go enjoy the rest of your life while the Universe is taking care of your business and providing you with the results you've requested, to the letter.

Until you get the hang of treating and releasing, it's not unusual for your mind to keep on chewing on the issue during the rest of the day. In that event, do something to stop the mental chatter and say something to yourself like, "I already took care of this." and kind of "pat the little doggie on the head" so it knows it's okay. Just continue to recognize the wholeness and "get offline."

If your mind is still chewing on the issue by the next day, you can do another treatment prayer if you choose, and then once again, "get offline." Keep doing your mental work daily until you're absolutely at peace about it. You'll know when you've done enough because your mind will wonder why you're even addressing this issue again since this was finished long ago.

- You made your divine connection and remembered to line yourself up with it.

- You realized your problem was no longer an issue and the old beliefs no longer had a grip on you.

- You released it to a universal law that's doing all the work on it.

How do you feel? Relieved? Elated? Happy? Joyous? Exuberant? Relaxed? Good. SAY SO! Declare "I feel so relieved and I'm finally relaxed. My whole body has just let go and I'm free to be happy and go have fun." Or "Wow! I feel so juiced that this opportunity is already mine!" It's just one more way of impressing your mind with your new state of being, and the Law of Mind is progressively more affected by your word.

PRACTICE TIME: RELEASE

Write sentences that affirm you are letting go of all this and letting the Law of Mind manage it.

_____

_____

_____

_____

_____

_____

_____

_____

_____

_____

_____

_____

_____

_____

_____

_____

Gratitude

> *If there is anything we need, it is peace of mind. Without it,*
> *life is not worthwhile. Peace of mind comes only when there*
> *is a personal and collective sense of security. This sense of*
> *security comes when there is a sense of belonging to the*
> *Universe. Jesus knew that no one is or ever can become suf-*
> *ficient to himself. It is when the soul returns to its source*
> *and finds its true center in pure Spirit that it enters into that*
> *peace which the Wise One said the world cannot give.*
>
> ERNEST HOLMES, *Words That Heal Today*

There's nothing like appreciation to make the world go around more happily. That's true of the Universe too. God loves appreciation. Haven't you noticed at home and at work that when you say thank you to someone, you automatically have a nicer relationship and the other person is suddenly more willing to be helpful and cooperative? The same is true for Spirit. It loves a thank you. Think about it. If someone had just asked you to do what you've just asked God to do for you, how would you feel if they didn't bother to say thank you? In the same way that the please's and thank you's are the grease in the cogs of life and make the world go around more smoothly, your gratitude is going to help create good results in your mental work.

Now that you're feeling terrific about your newly revised circumstances, be generous with your appreciation. Feel free to say:

"I'm so thankful this great job is already mine!"

"Thank you, Law of Mind, for making this already so. I'm so
    happy it's happening!"

"I'm grateful I don't have to think about this anymore. I can
    have my mental, emotional vacation!"

"Thank you, Spirit, for taking this off my shoulders. I couldn't
    have done this one alone."

"Hallelujah! The perfect solution is already here. Thank you, Lord, for saving this mess and inspiring me to a better way."

HERE'S A LITTLE TIP: If your life gets stuck and you're in a quandary as to how to fix it, a little gratitude goes a long way. Take pencil and paper at bedtime and every night write down ten things to be grateful for. If life is really trying and you can't think of ten new ones each time, use the old ones. Even if you're down to the simple things and you're grateful to have a bed, to be able to see, to be able to navigate stairs and you're grateful for the $2 you still have in your wallet, gratitude will improve your spirits and your circumstance. Try it. You're going to like it . . . a lot. It's a good practice for every day of your life.

It's a nice closing to this entire process to say something as simple as "Thanks, God" or more substantial like "I'm releasing this entire issue to the Law of Mind with great appreciation. I let go of this completely and I'm free. And so it is." More is not better—feeling and passion are better.

PRACTICE TIME: GRATITUDE

Write two or three expressions of gratitude.

_____

_____

_____

_____

_____

_____

Now write a couple of lines and put your *release* idea together with your *gratitude*. You might say something like, "I let go of this entire issue with enormous gratitude for the Law of Mind that has already made my request an outer reality."

CHAPTER 7

PUTTING IT ALL TOGETHER

Learn to live with the license of a higher order of being.

RALPH WALDO EMERSON

Congratulations! You have just successfully completed the most powerful healing process known to God and mankind. You now have all the tools to put your word out to the Universe to manifest what you want. Let's see how it sounds when all the parts are strung together.

To review, take your desire to the Universe/Spirit/Infinite Energy Field first and get yourself aligned with Spirit. Apply that truth to the problem. Throw out the negative beliefs and reaffirm the truth. Release it for Universal Law to work out, forget about it, and say thanks. That's it! Be sure to get the first two steps into the beginning of your re-visioning process. That's important. How much of Step Three (Specification) you include depends on how much ego fighting is happening and how much self-convincing you need to do.

Writing out your treatment/prayers may be easier while you are getting the hang of this process. As you keep adjusting your mind to think in this positive and productive manner, it will become automatic. Not only will you be declaring your truths out loud, you will be able to do them in your sleep, literally. One of the benefits to writing them is that you can keep them, and then one day when you need some clarity on that subject, you've already got it done.

As you write your treatment, you may state your truth for the person you are helping, or state it for yourself. If it's for someone else, you might say, "This treatment is for Betsy" and proceed to declare what is true about Betsy. If the treatment is for you, say, "This treatment is for me." And make statements about yourself and truth. You can also do your work in the first person for someone else, and it makes it very powerful, saying, "This treatment is for Betsy, and the truth I declare is for Betsy." Then you continue to do the work saying "I know this to be true," "I live my life with the license of a higher order of being," and continue in the first person. It's very powerful that way because when you hear the word "I" you are reminded that this is true for you too.

TREATMENT:

There was a treatment prayer for you earlier in the book for understanding of information. Let us do another to refresh your sense of flow between the steps. This one will be for intuition. Your first treatments may not be like this because it's all new to you. The ability and ease with the wording will come in due time. Just enjoy the benefits of this treatment, right here, right now.

This one Divine Intelligence, all-knowing, everywhere present, is being absolutely everything, everywhere, right now. There is only one Mind, knowing everything through all time and space. This universal Intelligence, being the reader, now has instantaneous access, in and through the reader, to every idea and experience relevant to doing the treatment prayer process. Every idea needed is instantly available. All the right intuitive and mental connections are already made. He/she has already gotten the hang of it and is already successful in using these techniques. Divine intuition brings forth the exact right ideas and associations to make these treatments highly effective. All doubts about what is right are now dissolved and replaced by great self-confidence and an inner light that radiates through the mind.

Every reader here now has the inspiration and enthusiasm to take this technique, use it, and light up their life.

This is true right now. This is my choice that I declare into the Law of Mind which now takes it and makes it so. It's not up for discussion. I release this declaration and know that this Law is now busy executing it perfectly in the minutest detail. I don't have to think about it anymore. It's all automatic from here. I let go of this idea with great thanks that it is already so. And so it is.

Great! You've just experienced your first treatment for yourself. Now it's time for you to write your own treatment.

Getting Started

Life will bring you pain all by itself. Your responsibility is to create joy.

MILTON ERICKSON, M.D.

Every person new to this technique of affirmative prayer feels a bit uncertain doing the first treatment by him/herself. The mind asks, "Where do I start? What do I say first?" That's why you had an earlier opportunity to write some phrases in each step. You've actually already done a whole treatment, so you really do know what to do.

The very first thing is to get quiet. If there is a quiet place available, find a comfortable place to sit and gather your thoughts. Sometimes, however, life gives us situations so quickly and with such speed that there is no time to do that, and you'll have to do your inner work on the spot in the middle of all the activity. At least take a couple of big, deep breaths to clear away the old energy and set fresh energy in motion.

Ask yourself "What is the problem here?" and answer it in one sentence. Make it to the point. What is the essence of the dis-order or the dis-ease to be changed? "I don't want to fail," or "I want my child to be healed." "My relative is dying," or "I'm scared I'll be really successful!" or "My husband needs $xxx to pay off the car by Friday."

Choose the positive, affirmative aspect of the situation. Out of all the qualities of the Infinite Intelligence, of God/Goddess and Spirit, which one(s) tie into the situation? Use these in order to make your first statements. Choose the aspect(s) of God/Goddess that you wish you had instead of what you're looking at. If the problem is fear, choose courage. If it's about being tired and having low energy, choose vitality and abundant energy. There's no need to worry about the appearance of the negative energies. Negative circumstances don't have any power on their own. They are the absence of Truth in that situation, so just choose the positive you'd like to create and the Law of Mind will carry it out. You can shift from:

Fear to fearlessness
Doubt to certainty
Lack to abundance
Not enough time to being on God's time, infinite time
Unhappiness to peace and joy
Limited circumstances to infinite possibilities
Job termination to new, expansive job opportunity
Sickness to radiant health
Loss to peaceful release
Fatigue, no zip to infinite, universal abundant energy
Pain to comfort, well being
Failure to success
Depression to vitality and passion

Whatever the problem, think of the opposite energy. What energies do you want? Go back to page 14 to expand your mind with the list of positive qualities of the Universal Spirit that's moving through you. See which of those qualities you would rather be experiencing. That's what you're going to call forth in your treatment/prayer.

You're ready to start your treatment with Step One, so take that quality you said you'd rather have in your life and remember it is Spirit. Remember to get Spirit in here first. Let's imagine you've got someone who's been dishonest with you. We'll name him Joe for the purpose of the example. You surely don't want any more dishonesty, so what *do* you want? Honesty and integrity.

SAY/WRITE:

> There's only One, one God, one Life, one Presence. It is perfect, whole and complete. Integrity is the nature of God. Honesty and integrity are here and available in their totality.

Step Two is to unite with that all-powerful, all-pervasive Spirit.

> Everything that is true of the Universe is true of Joe and me now. That means that the Universe as honesty and integrity are being me and my affairs right now. Because there is only one Mind, it's being my mind and Joe's mind as well. I don't have to do anything to make honesty and integrity happen or to make them available to this situation other than to call them forth. They are qualities of the Divine Presence and fill my life and affairs now. Honesty and integrity permeate every aspect of my relationship with Joe, no matter what has ever happened before. This is true NOW.

Step Three is where we get specific to the situation with Joe, the dishonest person in your life.

> No matter what Joe has told me or how many times he has lied to me, the truth about Joe is that he is made of God-stuff, and the nature of God is flawless honesty and integrity. I no longer take my cues and

information from the past. I'm not going to waste my energy guessing about the future.

Still not convinced? If you don't feel great about the situation yet, keep going in Step Three until you feel resolved and at peace about it all.

Joe lied to me because he was afraid. I can understand that. Everyone has fear from time to time. I now let go of my need to be right so that I can be happy. I tell my ego to give it up and I now make room for my love to flow. I don't have to like what he did, but I am willing to forgive him so I can regain my experience of peace. It's not about him. It's about my own sense of peace, and as I am at peace, I free him to his as well.

OK. We've gotten to a sense of peace now. So let's go on to Step Four, Release.

I'm giving this situation over to God and allowing absolute truth to fill it, renew it, restore it. It is not my responsibility to make Joe into a new person. My job is to see the divinity within him, to honor the God-stuff of his being, regardless of his inappropriate behavior. I now release this entire situation to the Universe, to the Law of Mind that now restores peace, balance and harmony between us. I'm not responsible for figuring out the details of what I'll say to him or what he will say to me, or when or where it will happen. Because I have chosen this in consciousness, the end is already guaranteed, so I don't have to sweat the middle part. I give great thanks for the healing of this relationship and am so happy to be able to move on in my life. And so it is!

PRACTICE TIME:

Here's where you get to try this out. Let's imagine your sister Tina needs $250 by Friday. The Universe doesn't care if it's for buying groceries, going to Tahoe for the weekend, or payment on her credit card bill. All the Law of Mind knows is that it's being requested to come up with $ 250 by Friday, right? So here we go. See if you can fill in at least two sentences for each Step.

Step One—Recognition (God first)

_____

_____

_____

_____

_____

_____

_____

_____

_____

_____

_____

Check to be sure you said something about Spirit being abundance or prosperity. (After all, Tina wants money, right?)

Step Two—Unification (It's Tina too)

_____

_____

_____

_____

_____

_____

_____

_____

_____

_____

_____

_____

_____

_____

_____

_____

_____

Did you say something about universal abundance is being her now? (Remember, there's _no future_. It's NOW!)

Step Three—Specification (What's true, what's not)

_____

_____

_____

_____

_____

_____

_____

_____

_____

_____

_____

_____

_____

_____

_____

You might have included ideas such as "Everything she needs is already provided," "I see her holding up a check for $250 on Friday." Or "No matter how nervous she is, this is the truth about her—the money is hers."

Step Four—Release and Gratitude (Let go and let the Law do it)

_____

_____

_____

_____

_____

_____

_____

_____

_____

_____

_____

_____

_____

_____

_____

_____

_____

Did you clearly declare you have let the situation go? "I get my hands off this and let the Law of Mind do its job," or "I release, let go and let God." And "THANK YOU!!"

Good job! Now read what you've written for Tina so you can hear your entire treatment flow out of you, because you've just done this treatment prayer all by yourself. The more you direct your mind to think in this way, the more effortless and spontaneous it becomes.

It might have come out in a simple form such as:

> There is only One Power, One Cause. It is unconditional abundance, prosperity and supply. Because this One Cause is everywhere, It's being Tina right now. No matter how challenging the circumstances appear, this One Source has everything she needs and supplies it now. Her identity is above the conditions; they have no power in her life. Tina's money is already here. Her needs are met. I see her happy, elated, and rejoicing, waving her $250 in the air! I let go of this treatment to the Law of Mind and am really delighted that she's at peace and her finances are already in order. Thank you, God! And so it is.

MORE PRACTICE:

Let us take your friend Harry, who's had a problem with an obnoxious neighbor, and write a treatment for them both to create a higher reality. Take a big, deep breath and quiet your mind. Ask yourself what it is they need. Now make the declaration, amongst your power statements about God/Life/Consciousness, that the Universe is being that too.

Step One—Recognition (Source first)

_____

_____

_____

_____

_____

_____

_____

_____

_____

_____

_____

_____

_____

_____

_____

_____

_____

_____

_____

_____

Did you remember that Spirit is love, peace or harmony? It might be that protection was a quality that seemed appropriate.

Step Two–Unification (Hey, it's being them too!)

_____

_____

_____

_____

_____

_____

_____

_____

_____

_____

_____

_____

_____

_____

Did you remember that God is being peace, not only as Harry, who needs the prayer, but as his neighbor as well? Does your sentence stay in the present, the now?

Step Three—Specification (Yea for the good news and down with the bad news)

———————————————————————————

———————————————————————————

———————————————————————————

———————————————————————————

———————————————————————————

———————————————————————————

———————————————————————————

———————————————————————————

———————————————————————————

———————————————————————————

———————————————————————————

———————————————————————————

You might have mentioned that because divine peace is being them now, and peace permeates the relationship with the neighbor, Harry can be at ease and finally relax and trust that the war is over. He now returns to a harmonious lifestyle. It's not appropriate for the mind to fret about imaginary next times. This treatment is true now and for eternity. The peace is his.

Step Four—Release and Gratitude

_____

_____

_____

_____

_____

_____

_____

_____

_____

_____

_____

_____

_____

_____

_____

Did you let go of this issue for them as well as you, and remember that the Law of Mind has guaranteed the harmonious results Harry needs?

Now read all four steps back to yourself ALOUD. Impress it on more than just one sensory organ of your being. You want to see it, hear it and feel the vibration of it in your body, your mind and your soul.

Great. You're getting the hang of it. This is usually the point in my workshops where the class members would like to hear how the entire treatment might sound. Here it is in the "beginner's version:"

> The only cause is Spirit, God. God's love is everywhere present, all the time, being right here as Harry, who needs this treatment, and the neighbor. Because Divine Peace is being them now, peace permeates the relationship and transforms it into harmony. No matter how many negative moments they've had before now, this treatment changes everything forever. Harmony and consideration are now at hand. I release this to the Law of Mind and it is done.

Here are two longer versions of the same treatment:

Treatment for Harmony

VERSION #1

> We all have the same Father. Our Creator is loving, patient, understanding and always available. He gave us an exquisite playground that we call Earth. The One who made us is pure consciousness, and He made us in His image. We are God being us on this plane. We all share the same Spirit nature, and we are one.
>
> Knowing that, we are one, my neighbor and I. I can now see that any trait I can identify in him is merely a reflection of my actions in my own life. I use this experience to examine where in my own life I am being obnoxious. I make amends. I forgive myself, and I ask for forgiveness, if to do so causes no greater harm. I become the kind of neighbor I want.
>
> I love that the Spirit in me listens and the Law responds by corresponding. I leave this treatment and allow the Law to do its work. With great humility and gratitude for this truth, I leave this treatment. And so it is!

> NANCY CALLAHAN, R.SC.P.

Here is another treatment for exactly the same obnoxious neighbor situation. See how two people can pray for the same thing and have two completely different approaches and still get the desired results? Everyone experiences Spirit in their own unique way, so naturally their treatments are going to reflect that uniqueness.

VERSION #2

I return to that still point within my being that is the Source of everything. It is the source of my mind and my every thought. From this center, I now realize that the only power in the Universe is God, Consciousness, pure Light. It is Love, and it is being both this man and his neighbor right now. This universal Presence is being pure love as these two people right now, regardless of how much fighting they've done to date. Love isn't interested in old fights. It's interested in the sweetness in the heart. This treatment now calls forth that sweetness in each of these people. Unconditional love is not attached to the circumstances of life. It doesn't care who did what to whom. It frees everyone to be the unique expression of God that they truly are.

So no one is trying to coerce anyone else anymore. The energies of being right and wrong are set aside. They are as nothing. Peace and harmony now appear in this relationship. A softness arises in their communications. The energies across the fence are more gentle now, and an inner permission is now given for each person to live their lives as they need to. The way of understanding and compassion is made clear.

The mind is not interested here in how they've treated one another in the past. The soap opera of the situation is not relevant to this new moment of creation. We are now ready to experience the not-yet-seen and the not-yet-heard in this relationship, and know that the light of Divine Love has now already descended upon them. The peace and the light of the Lord dwells within each of them, and it is apparent.

Now I sure as heck don't have a clue how to make this happen.

My only job here is to choose peace for this situation and release it to the Law of Mind which takes it and creates it in form. I don't have to understand the physics of it. I just know it works, A-1 guaranteed.

So I let go and quit thinking about it. It's in divine hands now, so I'm free to go about my business in absolute trust that these two people are experiencing a more harmonious interaction and peace.

I give great thanks that this is done unto me according to my word and is therefore already so. And so it is.

The point is not whether it is long or short, beginner's or experienced. The point is to know what you want, to choose it over your ego mind and emotions, and give it to the Law of Mind.

Treatment for Leg Problem

Here's a treatment/prayer written for a rash I had on my right leg. I knew the hot emotional topic of the time was about feeling stuck in my life and worrying about how I was going to make it. Here's what I wrote:

God is absolute unfailing protection, moving in me, as me, and through me, as protection from the erroneous identification with the world and specifically as protection from the effects of my old erroneous beliefs about what is possible. These legs move me forward in consciousness easily and effortlessly, and I am divinely carried to completion of all choices. The only effort I have to make is my conscious choice of aligning myself with God's love and support. I release the belief that I have to be able to heal myself. The Lord doeth all the work. I accept this Truth and rejoice in the instantaneous release of the old pattern. I no longer want it nor need it. It is now given to the Law of Mind and is already done. And so it is.

Needless to say, the rash went away because the source of it, which was irritation, was dissolved with the treatment.

In Conclusion

This is the process of effective, affirmative prayer, what Dr. Ernest Holmes called "treatment." It's one of the great phenomena of the Universe that works, no matter what you call it, no matter whose spiritual lineage you prefer.

Your thought is creative. The primary question is about your identity. Who do you think you are? Who is the "I" that you are using? If you are the "I" of Step One, the Infinite One, you are on track. You will manifest a higher truth, an unlimited potential, an infinite joy. If the "I" you identify with is the "I" of your conditioned, limited self, you will continue down the old path of disappointment. Every moment is a moment of choice. At every moment, you're at a crossroad. What do you choose for yourself now?

Every teaching of higher truth knows about creating out of the Infinite One. It's simple. You take your desire to the One, the creative matrix of consciousness. Put your attention on that receptive energy field, knowing that you and the Creative Power are the same. Declare your desire into the Universal Law, and watch it germinate and bloom into time and space. It works for everyone, regardless of one's history, status, story line or desire. It only needs your focused intention and enthusiasm, and your detachment from the results to change the forms of your reality. It is simply done unto you as you believe.

May your life be made anew. May you uplift others with your knowledge. May your knowledge be in service to Spirit and mankind.

> When your heart is in your dream, no request is too extreme.
>
> Jiminy Cricket

THINKING
FROM THE
INFINITE

PART TWO

CHAPTER 8

QUESTIONS AND ANSWERS

Life, nature and God only say "yes" to you . . . but what are you asking for?

Mark Victor Hansen

This section addresses many of the questions that often arise for people who are new to the treatment process, and offers refinements on effective prayer.

Q: Is this treatment/prayer process only a thinking thing? Isn't love important too?

A: Yes, Love! This book presents a technique that is primarily a manner of using the mind in the most effective manner for the greatest results. Treatment, in its "mechanical" nature, is indeed a thinking thing. In order to reverse the direction of energy that is already flowing, to effect change, you *have* to direct the mind in a consciously focused manner, with consistent, strong intention.

One of the beautiful and mystical things that occurs during the treatment is that your realizations and proclamations of truth begin to move energy from your head down into your heart, into the Sacred Heart, the center of your being. One has to start out with conscious thought and have an intention and a direction. However, usually by the time one has completed Step One, maybe Step Two, the energy has shifted and the practitioner has become immersed in the more refined energies of Love, Life, Goodness, Godness. The "treater" has arrived in the expanded state of correct identity with Source and begins to feel the love of the Universe flowing through him, and therefore through his thoughts and subsequently through his words.

The truth is that love is all there is, just like the song says. It is the love of God, the grace of the Master, that is the cause of everything that we can do as individual expressions of the One. The entire Universe is made up of love and grace. Surely by the time one gets to the gratitude section, that love is pouring out and the practitioner is already experiencing the grace that has taken over.

The treatment process begins in the mind and travels quickly to the heart. The sooner that occurs in the treatment, the quicker is the knowing that the work is already done. It sometimes transpires that you begin your declarations of recognition and become so impressed, so immersed in those qualities, that you forget why you were doing a treatment. The love and the bliss you experience is all you need for a realization of perfection. You're already "there," so there's no real need to continue.

Sometimes that occurs at the end of Step Two when the realization clicks in that you had forgotten that God was being you and the problem too. It's the realization that "I could have had a V-8." So when you've gotten it and felt the Ah Ha! of the new understanding, and your heart is happy, there may be no need to go on.

The rest of the treatment process is really to deal with the ego that is still trying to win out, trying to convince you that love isn't here and you're never going to be happy, and all those other ideas we struggle to overcome. You know you've overcome the problem when the love sets in. You've made the shift when you feel love, peace, and contentment, and there's only stillness left.

Use the mind to listen in silence and then declare what God said. Use the Law for specific results.

DR. BILL LITTLE

Q: When is the best time to do the treatment/prayer?

A: If life is happening very fast, or it is a case of emergency, do the treatment immediately. Don't wait until you get home or until life gets quiet. You may miss an important moment to make a difference and to heal a situation. It's nice to think we can always do our inner work in the quietude and privacy of our own space, but that is not always available to us. Sometimes we need to excuse ourselves from the party and go out on the patio, or find the men's room, sit in the car, or wander off somewhere to get a bit of space to focus our minds. In a moment of emergency, the focus of your mind is very important. Get it any way you can. Seize the moment and make that difference.

Given the normal pace of life, you may do your treatments any time you wish. Many people like to start their day by setting their intention for that day and also doing treatments for others who need it. Others prefer the time before bed because it clears out the debris of the day and leaves a serene mind for the night. After all, the thoughts you take to bed with you are going to grow and multiply overnight and you'll have MORE of them by morning. Therefore, be sure to release your day's issues before retiring. Treatment is ideal for this.

Q: How long do I treat for? Do I do this every day or just once?

A: The purpose of the treatment is for you to become crystal clear about the truth of the person or the situation. If you can do that in one shot, perfect. If you need to review the issue the next day, then do so. Keep doing your treatments until you are absolutely convinced that the condition or situation is healed and finished.

Any situation can be healed in one thought. Technically, the person who considers the problem and thinks "He's already healed," has just done her treatment in one sentence and doesn't need four steps. She's already convinced of the truth, and so she's experienced an instantaneous healing for the situation. Instantaneous healings are not extraordinary or improbable. They are par for the course for individuals who are focused and live at the center of their being.

The only reason that the treatment process includes four steps is because we often encounter situations that are either emotionally highly charged for us, or very complex, and we are confused. Regardless of our state, we use the steps of treatment to talk ourselves out of our confusion, attain clarity, make our choice for what we really want, and get on with our lives. This established sequence consistently allows one to be aligned with the One Source and Infinite Love.

Q: I learned that there are five steps to treatment. You only have four. Which one is right?

A: Everybody's right. As long as all the necessary information is there, it's right. The last two steps, Release and Gratitude, have been combined because the church I participate in uses four steps. The content is the same.

Q: How much money should I ask for? I have to have a couple hundred dollars, but I'd really like to win millions in the lottery. Should I treat for the millions?

A: The limit is not of the Universe. The limit is the finite concepts of the mind, and you'll not create more than the limits of your belief.

The purpose of treatment is not really to create more things or demonstrate more of something. It is to change our perception about reality, to align ourselves with the divine inner Truth, and to upgrade our beliefs about our relationship to the Universe as divine beings. We treat to expand our beliefs about identity. In doing that, we rise above the impact of experience in our lives and know a deep contentment within. Then our inner state automatically reveals itself in our outer world of form and experience.

Remember that you will manifest what you deeply believe. If you believe that you can only have a limited amount, that's what you will receive.

The goal should be realistic, a reasonable stretch of your faith. If you pray for ten million dollars and you have a ten dollar consciousness, you've overstretched your belief system. Yes, ask for more than your basic need. Ask for the plenty that is your divine inheritance. However, you'll want to stretch to something your mind can realistically believe. Otherwise, your *desire* will make the leap but your *belief* won't.

> *Begin with the possible; begin with one step. There is always a limit, you cannot do more than you can. If you try to do too much, you will do nothing.*
>
> P.D. OUSPENSKY AND G. I. GURDJIEFF

Q: Some of the treatments bring in other ideas besides just legs or just cancer. Where do these ideas come from?

A: Ideas that are dwelled upon for an extended period of time ultimately produce dis-ease. Some observable correspondences between mind and body have been made over the last century. They are called "mental equivalents" or secondary causation. We already know there is only One First Cause, so anything less than that is not, in truth, a cause to anything.

Here is an introductory list of some well-known associations between emotional states and body dis-ease. Remember that your intuition is always available to fill you in on what you should know at any given time.

Common cold = mental confusion
Allergy = over-sensitivity to life
Nose = spiritual discernment, discrimination
Asthma = smother love
Low back = financial or emotional support, focus on balance
Legs = moving forward in consciousness
Feet = understanding
Back = support
Arm = being able to embrace life, love, another person
Fingers = relating to the details of life
Heart = love
Liver = anger
Gall bladder =long standing hatred, usually a person or situation
Pancreas = attachment
Colon = the past
Kidneys = fear and anxiety
Large intestines = nervousness
Headache = too much thinking, mental overload
Baby's problem = a reflection of the mother's emotional state.

Q: I treated for my new idea to be successful. I told everyone what I was planning, so why didn't it work out? It all fell through.

A: What happened was that you leaked out the energy of your original excitement as you shared it before its time. What we don't need is too many people supervising the job at once. This is primarily because other people don't have your original vision, faith and energy for the activity.

When you let other people in on your new plans, they can only respond with their consciousness and ego. If some of those people are not visionary or supportive, they may tell you that you're not capable or qualified, smart enough, funded enough, artistic enough or anything enough to carry it through to the end. It is so easy for others to dump their fears, doubts, inadequacies and frustrations on you because if they can't do it, why should you? When we allow the negativities of others access to our vision, our enthusiasms can get dampened.

What's to do? You do your treatments to start the process. If someone asks what you're up to, you may tell them you have a new project but that you're not ready to discuss it just yet. Never mind that they will be just dying to know what you're doing. Stick to your original intention and protect it from people who want to pull up your visionary seedlings to see if they have sprouted yet.

Q: I asked for a specific kind of job, and I was banking on it. Instead I was offered something different that wasn't what I had in mind. What happened?

A: Either you had too much expectation or made an inappropriate choice. First of all, it is important to give Divine Intelligence enough leeway to be able to create for you the most appropriate job for your highest form of self-expression. Sometimes we think that our manifestation has to be just like this or that. However, if you've asked the

Universe for the *best opportunity* for you, you may not get your vision, but a Higher vision.

It's about the difference between expectation and expectancy. Expectation implies that it's got to turn out just so or you won't be happy. Guess what? You won't be, because you put such narrow parameters on the result that you'd never be happy anyway.

Our egos get all tied up in the form of the result. However, if we have an attitude of *expectancy*, an expectancy of Good, then the Universe can create something extraordinary, and, hopefully, we are happy to receive it. The expectancy of Good is looking forward with enthusiasm to what the Higher Mind knows we need, an excited anticipation instead of grasping anxiety about what is to be revealed.

My mother only gave me half the lesson. She'd say, "Don't expect so much and you won't be so disappointed." That kind of thinking got me YEARS of disappointments because I didn't dare set any goals or go for what my heart wanted. I didn't want to set myself up for the letdowns she predicted. She was exactly right! If you're dealing with expectation, you're pretty sure of getting let down when life does something other than your desire. When you ask the Universe and get specific, your demonstration may be exactly the same as your vision—or it may not. As Dr. Bill Little once said, "Don't close the door on your demonstration," meaning don't slam the door shut when the Universe is delivering your good just because your demonstration doesn't look exactly like your mental photograph. Trust that Perfect Intelligence is exactly that—perfect in its intelligence to give you your request in the highest form for your own good. Just tell your ego to get over it. Choose expectancy over expectation.

If you don't like what you created the first time, just make another choice and create the next reality. It's not hard. The same laws that brought the first choice into existence are still working and are ready to take your next request and make it so.

> *Be alert, be self-aware, so that when opportunity presents itself, you can actually rise to it.*
>
> DAVID BOHM

Q: I've been doing treatments for money for quite awhile and nothing is happening. Can you help me?

A: We need to have an honest look at your *belief* standing behind the treatment. The Law of Mind is going to create what you *believe*, to the letter. If your underlying belief is that you have no money, that's what you are going to create more of—no money. The poor get poorer. What needs to be adjusted is your belief that you have no money. Agreed there's no cash in the bank account, but that doesn't mean there's no money available. If you only consider the bank as a source, then indeed there is no money. The treatment is to change your belief about the source of money and how it relates to you.

Regardless of how many declarations you make, if you are immersed in poverty consciousness you will continue to reproduce that in your life. What's to be done? You go back to the first step of the process where you declare what is true about God/Goddess, Universe/Spirit. Get really juiced up about how vast, powerful, complete the Infinite Field of Consciousness is, how infinite Its prosperity really is. Impress yourself with the magnitude of what Infinite Abundance and Prosperity adds up to. Your mind can't even fathom that much wealth! Well, it's not enough that it's all out there and it's available to you. You've got to get it that it's all **being you now**, that you are God's abundance in action. Put **that** thought into the creative field of consciousness and into the Law of Mind.

Your job is to devote more time to redefining who you think you are. Are you the results of everything you've always believed, including "without money"? Or are you Divine Intelligence, Infinite Prosperity being you, just waiting for you to give up your old, erroneous identifications so It can give you everything It has in store for you? It is the Father's good pleasure to give you the Kingdom of Heaven. It's time we quit saying we're not worth it and started revising our beliefs to fit the Truth. A fast track to shifting your identity? Start meditating, and then you'll begin to know from the inside out who you really are. Amen!

Q: Is it OK to treat for my friend? She's having such a hard time. I know it would help her a lot.

A: Absolutely. Every declaration of Truth we state is an upliftment to the entire world. Any time you pronounce the Truth for someone, your declaration uplifts them, transforms them and indeed alters the cosmos.

Once in awhile, we encounter someone who really doesn't want to be healed. That person may have an emotional investment in their dis-ease. It may be that they get attention from others or that they are trying to make others as unhappy as they are. If you've done your inner work on behalf of someone who is not improving, it's likely that they are not ready to give up their ego-motivated behavior. You can always treat them to a motivation that comes from Love.

Q: I asked for the perfect partner in my life and I got somebody who has a lot of disappointing qualities I didn't ask for. What went wrong?

A: You asked for the perfect partner. She must be perfect for the you that you are today, otherwise she wouldn't be here. She may be the ongoing manifestation of the kind of person you usually attract because your new vision of a partner has not had enough time to take hold in your consciousness. Treat again and hold your new vision firmly in your mind.

You may opt to do a new treatment and choose again. We don't make bad choices. Maybe uninformed, inappropriate, or unconscious choices, but there aren't any bad ones. No "dissing" on yourself, and no "should-ing" on yourself. You just make a new choice and go forward. The Law of Mind will be perfectly happy to create your next reality.

This may also be a matter of not having had everything on your shopping list. When you're "shopping" for something (someone) in your life, be descriptive. Otherwise, it's like walking into Macy's with a

$100 bill, standing at the bottom of the escalator and calling, "Hey! I want to buy something." They will think you're weird and you won't get any service. Now, if you wave your $100 bill and yell out "I need new shoes" you'll be directed to the shoe department, and you'll have your needs met.

This time you might focus your shopping list with qualities such as honesty, wise use of money, intelligence, sense of humor, patience, relationship to pets, lifestyle, personal hygiene, sexual interest, and so on. You'll get what you ask for down to the last detail. If your lady still fits the bill, she'll stay; otherwise, someone new will show up. It's your choice.

Q: I've been praying that my daughter would marry this man before the baby arrives. She's rebelling and not going to get married.

A: It isn't working because you are praying in an attempt to get somebody else to do something that YOU think is right. That, my dear, is pure ego insisting on having its way. Spirit doesn't do ego. It manifests for the highest and best for all concerned. If marriage isn't the highest and best for your daughter, the father of the child, and the child, it "ain't happenin'." It is possible that underlying beliefs from your past do not fit the truth for these people. They have their own destinies. It is not your issue, even though you think it is. You are related to them, but they have their own lives, with their own life scripts, lessons and journeys to get there. The prayers are not "working" because you are trying to tell the Universe what is right, and to make it so in form. Ooops.

What would be more effective is to ask that the most appropriate living arrangement be created for the common good of the new "family," an arrangement that brings love, harmony, joy, consideration and support to each person in the family unit. That way, Universal Intelligence can devise a setup that actually works better for them than what you wanted. Quite simply, when we pray and ask for goodness, we have to get our egos out of the way.

We need to give up what is called "do-ership"—the notion that we of ourselves can, must, and will do something. But "I of myself do nothing. It is the Father within that doeth the work." We have to release what we think we want and be willing to accept a higher solution. The amazing thing is that when you release your attachment to the solution and ask for the highest good of all concerned, you get exactly what you need as well.

W e can speak so confidently about the outcome of all your human problems because we know that all human life is governed by a divine law, perfect in its outworking. The purpose of that law is to draw all men and women, all the human family, into a consciousness of God. Do not look backwards unless it is to say, "How beautiful the path that I have traversed!" Do not regret the past. You are moving forward, traveling life's path to find happiness once again, and this time an enhanced happiness.

CARELL ZAEHN

Q: I've been getting treatments done for my father who has cancer, but it looks like he's still going to have to have chemotherapy and radiation. Isn't the treatment working?

A: The truth is always true. The treatments know that your father is healed now, in whatever form that may need to manifest for his highest good, and you're not the boss of that. Remember that it's our beliefs that manifest through us. If your father believes that he'll only be healed by receiving chemotherapy and/or radiation, then that's the way the healing is going to come. You can treat that *his* beliefs expand to be able to accept an instantaneous healing. *You* can do the work *for* him to be able to accept instantaneous healing. The healing is already done on the higher plane, and the Divine is waiting for us to open the door wide enough to let It in.

Perhaps this person is at the end of his life span, regardless of whether he is 45 or 95 years old. An Intelligence that is infinitely wise, loving, good, kind and benevolent knows when the life script is up, regardless of our impending loss. It is important to let God do Its job. It is possible that your father's work here is finished, irrespective of your opinion and limited worldly vision. It may actually be for his highest good to move on so he can start his next phase of soul growth. Your job is to see the perfection in his spirit, his progress, to know the right thing is happening for him. Treat him for peace. Treat *yourself* for peace so you can get out of God's way and let the healing happen, whatever that means.

Perhaps what is needed is your unconditional love, love that has *no opinions*, just love. sweet, caring, unending love. No scripts, no history, no expectations, no story line and no "shoulds," from him or from you. Then you are both free to just BE, and now you're on track. As you make this shift, you're both free, and the best and the highest happens easily.

Q: Is it true that you have to get rid of your old beliefs before you can expect a new life?

A: Yes and no. Life is a process, a journey. For most people, we let go of our old habits and ways of thinking a little at a time. Nevertheless, you can't wait till the old is gone to start building your new experience. Begin today to hold that vision of the new you. Make your conscious , clear choice for the new. Declare the old finished, obsolete. Then get out of the way and let the shift happen in God's perfect timing. Yes, participate in those techniques that help clear out the wrong understandings, old impressions. It helps to empty your cup of the old so you can fill it up with more of the new. I received a sweet plaque as a gift that said, "Be patient. God isn't finished with me yet." You do your treatments for the new you *and* you are patient with the process.

Q: I'm not always sure if my request is coming from ego. Do you have any thoughts?

A: Just ask yourself, "Is this an ego thing I'm doing?" You'll get a definite answer. If you even had to ask the question, the answer is "yes."

You can use treatment to get what you want and to manipulate circumstances for ego reasons. A more beneficial inner stance is that of service.

As Dr. Bill Little says, "If you are in service to the Universe, you will never have to worry." As Albert Schweitzer said, "I do not know what path in life you will take, but I do know this: If, on that path, you do not find a way to serve, you will never be happy."

When you are in service, you are out of ego. In India, it is called *seva*, selfless service. It is one of the primary spiritual practices for eliminating the ego's grip and instilling more refined states of consciousness. In true service, there is an understanding of the whole, the bigger picture, and a benevolent attitude of helpfulness, of givingness to the Whole. That is why many people in treatment like to include a phrase like, "This or something for the good of all concerned," "This or something better." If the purpose of doing your treatment/prayer work is for wholeness or for the upliftment of others, you are on track and your work will produce wonderful results.

Q: Why do all the treatment/prayers have "and so it is" at the end?

A: It's very much like the "Amen" in the Christian tradition, or the "Swaha" in the Hindu faith. They are all phrases declaring completion that include the concept of release. None of them are required, but add the grace note for a nice, clean ending.

Summary Thoughts

- We aren't treating to get someone else to become something other than their divine perfection.
- We never manipulate another's behavior.
- If your desire is great but your faith is thin, your manifestation will need some support.
- Treat to grow your faith.
- If you don't like what you created the first time, create something else.
- Be specific, but not endless in your details.
- Hold an attitude of expectancy rather than an expectation.
- Don't slam the door on your demonstration. God may have a better idea!
- Protect your new vision until it's had time to sprout and grow strong.

Every disorder seeks order;
all dis-ease can find ease.
In partnership with God,
we can call forth
the divine healing capacities within
to work in every area of our lives.
Our bodies are precious gifts
designed to house our holiness.

MARY MANIN MORRISSEY

CHAPTER 9

TREATMENTS FOR MIND, BODY, AND SPIRIT

Expect your every need to be met. Expect the answer to every problem. Expect abundance on every level. Expect to grow spiritually.

Eileen Caddy, *The Dawn of Change*

The following treatments are provided so that you have available a number of clear treatments for the variety of circumstances you may be presented with. They address many commonly encountered situations and needs of life on the planet. There are treatment prayers for material needs, health issues and spiritual qualities. Please use them for inspiration or as needed for yourself and others.

For a wide variety of "flavors," I've included treatments from individuals who are spiritually adept at treatment/prayer work. It helps you to realize that your treatments are just perfect the way they are, because The Truth is always Truth, regardless of through whom It flows.

WORLD PEACE

No matter what is going on in the world, it is not cause. The only cause is First Cause, Infinite Intelligence, Divine Wisdom and Perfect Peace. This One Power, Universal Creative Presence is everywhere present through all time and space, and that means NOW. God isn't going to become more effective or more present or more powerful later on. This is happening right here, right now, through and as every human being on the planet. This One Mind is being each and every soul in existence and this Perfect Peace moves in and through each of them right now.

Regardless of the dramas of the world, I now consciously choose the immediate manifestation of world peace. No matter what a civilization's background is or what a country's belief system is, within every soul is the one thread of Spirit, wholeness, and respect for one another. I invoke this mutual respect now. I choose a planetary consciousness of unity, a singularity of purpose, an honoring of each individual's inalienable rights and beliefs. Where there has been suspicion of differences, I choose appreciation for the common ground of all. Where there has been a history of war, I choose an expanded understanding that includes peace. Universal harmony is available here and now, and I choose it for the entire planet.

This is my declaration unto the Law of Mind which has received my word and shall not return it unto me void. The Law has got its new instructions and the end is guaranteed. With great gratitude, I release this treatment and rejoice now in the peace that is already here. And so it is.

CARELL ZAEHN

PEACE OF MIND

This is the moment I turn away from the outer circumstances and remember there's a higher choice. I recognize that there is but one Power, one Intelligence, one Cause, one Source. This one Cause, whether it is God, or Spirit or Buddha or whatever it is, I know it is peace. This peace is the Source and Cause of my being, breathing me and beating my heart. It is what not only moves my body through this life, it is the basis of all my affairs. I now take this time to remember that it is the foundation of my whole life.

I now shift my investment in my problems to an attention within. I realize that all the power I was giving to my issues belongs on the One Source. I could have been having a better experience. Well, I choose it now. I'm not going to judge myself for having forgotten my true Source and Power; I just tune in and accept it now. As I accept my correct inner Source, I now have the instantaneous experience of inner peace. I turn all my issues over to the Infinite Intelligence that knows exactly how to rearrange them for my highest good. Now that I don't have to figure everything out myself, I relax and enjoy the peace that is here and available for me at every moment.

I accept this inner peace as a lifestyle. No more worry habits that try to tell me God can't handle my affairs. No more negativities because I forgot to have a spiritual V-8. I now live, move and have my being in perfect peace, the peace that passes understanding.

I give this treatment to the Law that has answered by request already. There is nothing to do but enjoy this inner quietude that is mine. And so it is.

CARELL ZAEHN

RELEASE FROM FEAR

There is nothing "out there" which is not made of God stuff. The same energy that created me creates absolutely everything else. This one Creator is an energy of loving kindness, protection, and safety. God's all-pervasive protection and security surround me now and I am filed with strength and fearlessness. Because Spirit has made everything else in the One, whatever it is that I have been fearful of now knows that I have changed my inner stance to one of fearlessness and the attack is off.

I am a warrior of the divine. No one can take anything away from me, make me less than I AM. No one can cause me sadness, loss, depression, or fear because they are not cause in my life. I take my power from a higher order of being. I am not afraid to take drastic actions if they are required. Because all my actions are motivated by my connection to the One Mind and the One Power, I cannot make a mistake, I cannot hurt another in my fearlessness, nor can they hurt me. My power comes from within and I use it to affirm right action, truth, and respect for myself and for others.

Nothing in the world can keep me in pain or deprivation because God is my source and my supply. Nothing ever goes wrong in the universe, no matter what things look like in the instant. God has a better idea and is at work implementing the plan on the grand scale. Just because I can't see the bigger picture at the moment doesn't mean I don't trust it. I KNOW that everything is NOW working out in my favor. I know it, I accept it, I trust it, and I give thanks for it.

So this treatment is now released to the Law of Mind. My peace of mind is now here and I'm feeling at ease and protected.

That's a relief! And so it is.

Carell Zaehn

IN CASE OF AN ACCIDENT

OK, I now shift gears quickly to remember that in this instant there is only one Power, one Presence, one Peace. It is right here, right now and It's being X right now. All of divine Intelligence is right here, knowing exactly how to stabilize this person and restore their body to perfect balance. This One, perfect Intelligence directs me to be helpful in appropriate ways, even though I may not consciously know what they are, and I KNOW that perfect Intelligence is at work and has everything under control.

All the right help is now available. This person is cared for immediately in the highest manner possible. They get the best medical care available. Divine Intelligence is operating in and through every medic and physician that comes to assistance. Every medical move is perfectly executed in divine order and wisdom for x's highest good.

I declare a sense of peace and comfort for this person. In the One Mind, they realize that all is now well and are able to surrender to the flow of what's transpiring and to the help that is being brought to them. They, too, now know the peaceful Presence in their life.

OK, Law of Mind. It's your ballpark. Take care of it. THANK YOU! And so it is.

CARELL ZAEHN

PERFECT HEALTH

The only cause to anything is the One, Perfect, All-wise, Ever-present Source. It is the source of my mind, my body, my emotions. My health comes from my awareness of God/Goddess living me, breathing me, renewing me. God in me, as me renews me now in body, mind and spirit to reflect the wholeness of pure Being.

I welcome the flow of Spirit through my body, restoring every cell to perfect balance I invite Wisdom to assist me in choosing the right foods and the right lifestyle for optimum health for this body. I give attention to how I eat and live and how my outer health contributes to my inner health. I am aware of the outer influences in my life and how they affect my inner balance. As within, so without. My inner health and outer health are one.

Perfect health is mine now. I take my information and directions about my health from Spirit, not from the comments or opinions of others. I am renewed every moment by the energy that flows within me because it is the very essence of God.

This is the truth. This is my declaration unto the Law of Mind, that fertile field of receptive energy that now takes my word and makes it so. With great appreciation, I release this treatment. And so it is!

CARELL ZAEHN

PERFECT WEIGHT

There is only One, One Love, One Light, One Source. This One is the source of Infinite Perfections made manifest in all dimensions including Mind, Body and Spirit. This One is Absolute Abundance, Pure Joy and Pure Love. This One is unlimited in its ability to radiantly and joyously express its perfections and wholeness at all times and in all ways. This One is All-Encompassing and Truly All That Is.

This One is now, at this very moment and at all moments, expressing as me. I am one with this source of Infinite Perfection made manifest in all dimensions, including Mind, Body and Spirit. I, as this One, am unlimited in my ability to radiantly and joyously express my perfection and wholeness at all times and in all ways.

Because I am One with All There Truly Is, I now fully accept by divine birthright and allow myself to fully express as the radiant being of perfection that I am. It is totally safe and totally acceptable for me to now express as physical, mental and emotional perfection. My body, as the physical manifestation of the Divine in me, functions in perfect synchronicity with all aspects of my life. My physical body now effortlessly and easily reaches the perfect weight and appearance for me as a unique individualized soul expressing in physical form. I rest easily, knowing that all of the components necessary for me to achieve my own unique form of physical perfection are already known to me and will be revealed to me at the appropriate and best moment. I exude health and vitality, and I manifest abundant, unlimited energy and joy.

I bless this overall process with love, and I now "let go and let God" handle all the details of accomplishing this Treatment for me. For this I am truly grateful. And so it is.

CATHY COLE

ELIMINATE DEPRESSION

The outer world is not cause. I turn my awareness back to the one Creative Power, Divine Enthusiasm, to Life because it is the source of my life. Creative Power and Divine Enthusiasm are being me, being my life here and now. My life isn't going to get better sometime later. There isn't any later; there's only now and I now choose to put the zing back into my experience.

The one infinite Universal Mind is not stuck for solutions. It is never trapped by outer circumstances. Because Divine Mind is infinite, it has the perfect set of solutions to move me out of stuck-ness and forward into enthusism for life and for my perfect self-expression. This is the moment that I quit giving all my power to the events of the world, to the circumstances in my life. Yes, they are happening, but they are leftovers of previous thinking. They area not cause. THIS is the moment of new thinking and creating new effects in my life.

I now consciously choose an increased sense of freedom, lightness of being, joy, enthusiasm for life. I choose to be excited about my gifts and my talents that are unique to me and I choose to get them up and running and out into the world. This may mean I make a paradigm shift in my life. My outer experience may change substantially, however, I trust the wisdom of Infinite Intelligence completely to restore my energy, my enthusiasm and my inner light.

I'm turning all this over. All of it. My entire life is now turned over to Spirit for renewal, regeneration and rebirth. Now I'm excited to see just how inventive Universal Intelligence can be. It surely won't be any solution I've come up with yet, so it's going to be a really good one! I let go and let God manage my life and my affairs from here on. Now that's a relief!

So, Law of Mind, you know what to do. Now do it. Rearrange my life so I experience the joy of the divine in it. That's your job, and I get my attention off it now and let you do your work. And so it is.

CARELL ZAEHN

LOVE

We know that there is only One, One God, One Creator, One Source of all that is. We know that God is everything. This sweet One, this precious One is breathing me and being me right now.

I am unconditional love personified, for God is me. I accept and give love easily as loving is who I am. I am trusting, compassionate and open to the love in my world. I allow love to be the foundation of my life.

I invoke the Law and know that it is in operation at all times and I am grateful that it is so.

NANCY CALLAHAN, R.SC.P.

RIGHT RELATIONSHIP

Let's go back to Source. One Cause, First Cause. It is pure Consciousness, Divine Intelligence. It's being absolutely everything, no holds barred. That means it's being me now. It's being me, my life, my relationships, everybody I know and everybody I don't even think I know. This One Perfect, all loving Presence loves me completely, more than my finite self is capable of perceiving. This one loving, all-caring Presence now fills my life with the perfect relationship for my happiness, my growth and my needs. Because I am loving to myself, I attract a partner who loves me in kind. Because I respect myself, I attract a partner who respects me. I know that I attract a person who is aligned with my values and beliefs, a person who is a reflection of my beliefs. This person is already perfect, and corresponds to who I truly am.

And so I see my perfect partner already here, in loving relationship. It is already done as I believe it and see it, and I see us together now. I release this treatment to the universal mind which has already produced the experience and I wait with great expectancy as the manifestation unfolds. And so it is.

CARELL ZAEHN

FRIENDS AND COMPANIONS

One Source, one Cause, one loving Presence which knows Itself as friendship. This is a friendship that manifests itself in my world as friends and companions who are good company. Because God's presence is always here in my life as friendship, I know I always have personal friends and companions that are a reflection of this inner friendship. They are joyous, nurturing, supportive. They are good listeners as well as inspiring in their ideas and actions. Because there is only One Mind, they are not only a reflection of God but they are a reflection of me as well.

Regardless of the changes that occur in my life, no matter how many times I relocate or where I travel, I am surrounded by positive companions and dependable friends. I don't always know where they come from. I just know that they are always available. The right ones are there at the right time for the right reason. That's the nature of divine Friendship. It's "God company" and I love it.

I feel very nurtured and supported to have ongoing happy friends and associates and I am most grateful for their presence in my life.

I release this treatment to the Law and it is absolutely so. And so it is.

CARELL ZAEHN

FAMILY HARMONY

Love is the nature of the Divine. Because the One, First Cause and all of Creation is made of love, that means that no only is my nature love, but it is true of everyone. Specifically, my family is made of that loving God-stuff.

No matter how inappropriately someone has behaved or how insensitive someone is being, it is not who they are. Just by my now remembering the truth of their being, this loving nature which is who they really are now reveals itself. My family functions as an integrated loving whole, sensitive, warm, nurturing, and respectful. Each individual moves in harmony with another in joy, light and consideration. Never mind what they say, my word is now spoken into the Law. It is spoken by God, through God, and for God for Its perfect revealment as loving harmony in my family. This is my choice and I release it to the Law, and it is done. And so it is.

CARELL ZAEHN

NEW HOME

Everything I need is contained in Universal Wholeness, perfect Wisdom and Divine Intelligence. There is only One Mind happening and It's everywhere, through all time and space. Everywhere means It's being me now. Right here, right now, the entire focus of the Universe is laser beamed in on my request for the perfect new home.

I choose a wonderful home on the Monterey Peninsula in Carmel or Carmel Valley, in a warm spot with lots of sunlight, great trees and open space, a house with huge windows or the ability to create huge windows. And it's cute with ample land and an extra room for me to paint and create! I choose nice neighbors that allow me the privacy I need to live my lifestyle. I choose a neighborhood that is safe and protected for myself, my family and my pets. I have easy access to getting to the supermarket, to classes, to my clients. The price is absolutely perfect, and the financing arrangements are effortless. The Universe can afford this house by means of me.

Any real estate talk that it's too expensive to buy property on this Peninsula is spiritual B. S. It's flat out not true. It is the Father's good pleasure to provide me with a beautiful home to live in, with a magnificent setting as well. And so I accept my new home. I see myself choosing it, moving in, decorating it, planting my favorite flowers in the yard. I see my cats frolicking in the garden. It is perfect!

The money is perfect too. That means the price and the financing—it's all in God's hands to create this, and it is created simply because I have envisioned it and chosen it. I keep my attention fixed on the goal. There is no negative idea from anyone, especially from myself, that can sway my sights. My vision is fixed.

So, Law of Mind, you've got the information. It's your job to turn it into form, in every last detail. I release this treatment with much love and appreciation. And so it is.

CARELL ZAEHN

FOR A CHILD

There is just ONE Source, ONE Light, ONE Energy. That ONE is God, Good, Love. That perfect source of knowing is being this child now. Every cell and molecule are alive with this truth. How I perceive this child is clearly changed by this realization. The truth is present and the path is clear.

I release all the old identifications I have held about this little being and know this is the truth of this person NOW. I choose for the wisdom of the Universe to transform the situation at hand and I choose it now. All is now resolved in love, harmony, compassion and understanding, and I'm feeling much better already because this is true. The previous behaviors have no more power. Those energies are now dissipated and replaced by peaceful cooperation.

So I let go of this treatment, knowing that it is perfect and it will unfold for his/her highest good. And so it is.

PAM GEORGE, R.SC.P.

SURVIVING DIVORCE

This is the moment I shift my attention from what seems to be going on in the world and put it onto First Cause, the One Power, the only Source. This one Power is Unconditional Love, right here, right now, and It's being me now. It's being me, my life, my partner and my family. Love is the truth of everyone and all the movements in my life, regardless of appearances. I'm not living my life based on appearances and circumstances. I live my life from the center of my being which is perfect Love, Light, Wisdom, Serenity, and Wholeness. No matter how the world swirls around me, I am peacefully planted at the center of my being where everything is taken care of in perfect right order.

God's love in me and as me is complete, absolute. That means that my sense of being loved does not come from others, including my mate. Feeling loved springs from my own heart. The love I want and experience emanates from me. The people around me are a reflection of the love I am recognizing within my being.

This perfect, divine Love as me cannot be diminished by someone else's acceptance or rejection of it. It is complete and ever-full, overflowing in my being and my life right now. There's no such thing as a shortage of love. Any fears or thoughts I had, or that my friends had, about being in a negative situation with this divorce are shoved aside. I have no time for that kind of thinking. I insist on seeing love radiating in every aspect of my life experience. No matter how disappointed I may feel that the relationship isn't continuing, I know that the Universe has a divine plan for me and that my next experience is already a great one. God only taketh away to replace it with something even better, and I am now open and happy to receive it.

I surrender to the Infinite Wisdom of the Universal Order in my life and know that perfect relationship healing is now taking place. Now, the Law of Mind has got my directions. This is my Word. It is done by God, as God, for God, and my Word cannot come back to me void. It is released with gratitude and a huge sigh of relief. And so it is.

CARELL ZAEHN

CREATIVE EXPRESSION

This Universe and everything in it is the creative expression of an exquisite Intelligence. Called by many names, It is Spirit. It is the only Source of all manifestation. It makes everything out of Itself by becoming the thing it makes! It is everywhere present, all of it, all the time, all at once!

This means that my mind and my life are right now arising out of all that Spirit is. With each breath I draw in its life force. With each exhalation I express its essence. With each thought I access its field of creative possibilities. My mind is its advent into manifestation. I say "Spirit, use me!" There is an immediate response, as if Spirit were saying to me, "Use what I am!"

Knowing that my creativity is an outlet for Spirit to reveal itself in the time space dimension, I let it rip! I trust ideas to spring up in my mind and to have within them the power to move me into action. I know that as the acorn contains the oak tree, my ideas are filled with Spiritual know how.

I can never run out of ideas because I can never use up the Infinite field of possibilities that Spirit is. I accept my creative nature and let it live through me.

Grateful that I am so able to serve, I say. And so it is!

REVEREND CAROL CARNES
CENTER FOR CONSCIOUS LIVING, SANTA CRUZ CA

PURPOSE IN LIFE

The only life there is is the One, One Life, one loving Presence, God/Goddess, Pure Consciousness. It is being me , my life, my mind, my goals, my purpose. This one omniscient Power for Good knows exactly how my life needs to unfold and unfolds it now in perfect love and order.

It is only my ego sense of control that thinks it's got to be in charge, figure everything out, make the best decisions and not mess up my life. It's not my life! It's GOD'S LIFE! God isn't messing up Life, and that applies to my life as Its supreme individual expression of Perfect Being.

That means I can now relax, surrender to the Infinite Loving Presence that re-creates me, re-arranges my life and always has me in exactly the right place at the right time for everything I need. All my needs, wants and concerns are already met and provided for. I allow my life to unfold according to a higher plan. That means I am sensitive and receptive to the opportunities that come my way. I am open to new thinking, new experiences, new places. I surrender my attachment to how I think things should be and get in line with what the Universe knows is for my highest unfoldment. Whatever that is is already perfect. I am now willing to listen within to hear what that is and to accept my good as it arrives.

My life unfolds in a joyous magnificence. I feel completely at peace about it all and am ready to move into the next exciting phase.

Thank you, God, for this moment of remembering what's really going on here and for enabling me to get out of my own way.

I release this treatment to the Law, which is working automatically, providing everything I need for my life's self-expression NOW. And so it is.

CARELL ZAEHN

NEW JOB OPPORTUNITY

The truth is that the Universe has got everything together. All of Divine Intelligence is always on top of every situation, and that includes this one. This One is perfect self-expression, perfect employment as service to the world. All employment is an expression of the Divine Self, and as we offer our abilities in service to others, we receive every blessing we need. This One Intelligence is in me, right now. His mind is a channel for the One Mind to flow into and through his life, directing him to the perfect opportunity for his self-expression and his prosperity. There is no gap in God's unending love and caring for Its child, and this child of the Universe is not left alone or left without. If a child asks its father for a loaf of bread, will he give him a stone? And so the Divine Father now provides absolutely. That means ongoing income at the level to which he's accustomed, good people to work with and for, joyous self-expression on the job, all the equipment necessary to fulfill the responsibilities.

It doesn't matter what the circumstances look like at this moment. The Universe creates anew at every instant. New opportunity is created out of this instant, from this still, quiet place within, from which all thought arises.

And so I release this request to the Law of Mind which is automatic in its delivery. It doesn't think about it, rationalize, evaluate facts or any of that mental stuff. It simply takes the choice and rearranges the Universe to make it so.

So here's to my new job. It is perfect in its scope, its income, its duration, with the perfect people for the perfect reason. I'm grateful to this Law for already making this opportunity so, and grateful that he's so pleased with the outcome. It's terrific! And so it is!

CARELL ZAEHN

SUCCESS IN BUSINESS

We always go back to the source of all, the One, all-pervasive and abundant Supply. It is Prosperity. It is Success. It is Self-Expression in the world as service, and it is in me right now. My entire career and business enterprise is supported and directed by this one prosperous Intelligence that knows exactly how to bless and prosper. All my affairs are imbued with the Infinite's desire to reveal success and prosperity. Abundance of energy, enthusiasm, competence and self-expression are all present in my activities. Because my work is service to the world, I have prospered to the max. I now attract money like a magnet. People want my services. People value my services and want to pay for them.

I now release all my old projections of money and success and step into my real identity now as an individual expression of the One Self. My identity of Self is now altered to a higher vibration. I am now free to be the perfect embodiment of Self in my career. It's not work. This isn't hard. It's about knowing that my joyous self-expression is what God wants to pay for, and so I let myself go all the way into the expansion that is available with astonishing success. I am a highly successful person, doing what I do best, expressing my own gift to others.

I let go of this treatment. There's nothing else to be said. It is perfect and so it's off to the Law of Mind which has already made it so. And so it is.

CARELL ZAEHN

RIGHT ATTITUDE

There is only One, perfect Consciousness, divine Intelligence, pure Wisdom, being all in all, at every point in the Universe simultaneously. It is everywhere right now and that means in me, as me, and through me. The mind I am using is the One Mind, the Divine Mind. I see my world through the eyes of a higher order of Being.

That means that my attitude is of that same higher order of Being. My thinking is now readjusted to perceive people and situations the way that God sees them. I am willing to release my limited mind-set and allow Spirit to think through me and respond rather than react through me. My attitude now knows that anything is possible with Spirit. Not only am I now open and available to all possibilities, I also open to the attitudes of love, compassion, nurturing, tolerance, patience, consideration and all the more uplifting attitudes I may not have used for a while.

No matter how I may have been challenged with people at work or family situations, I am in tune with Divine Right Attitude and the attitude of gratitude. I appreciate all the goodness that flows through my life. I am grateful for the gift of a human body and a mind that can contemplate its own divinity. I release my old tendencies to negative and critical thinking and now am in the flow of an expansive and uplifting attitude. Not only does it bless my mental state, it is a gift to my mind/body/spirit connection and to everyone around me. I'm through being a drag on myself and others and now move into a joyous, appreciative, positive mode where now all the really wonderful things of life can happen.

It is my choice to operate in right attitude. And so into the Law of Mind it goes and it is now done unto me. Hey, this is great because I'm not stuck anymore! And so it is. Yea!

Carell Zaehn

PROSPERITY

I'm going back to First Cause for my true identity with Prosperity. The source of all wealth, affluence and money is God, not my bank account, or my parents, or my job. Universal Wholeness is my Source, and that Source of wholeness and perfection flowing through my life now. It provides me with all the funds I need to take care of my obligations and my enthusiasms as well. Money is a vehicle for the expression of my very Self in the world, and since it is sourced by God and Infinite Supply, there is never any shortage of it, for me or for anyone else.

I now choose a dramatically increased flow of money into my daily life and an all-around prosperous experience. I choose it from the infinity of possibilities. I am willing to consider that everything I have been taught to believe about prosperity and affluence may be untrue, regardless of how well-meaning the intentions of others. I am willing to be as giving to others and to my world as my desire is to receive. I am willing to look at my concept of my own self-worth to see if that is why I have not been receiving my abundance. I am willing to ask myself if my work is stifling my joyous self-expression. Am I working because I have to, or am I living my passion?

I invite this infinitely intelligent and compassionate Presence to reveal to me just where and why I may have cut off my own flow and to show me how I can participate in the expansion of my own wealth experience. I welcome all the wisdom of the Universe to re-teach me about wealth, to modify my attitudes and beliefs, and to align me with the supreme truth of wealth and affluence.

This is my declaration unto the unified field of pure Consciousness, this pulsating, scintillating field of energy that is taking my choice and moving it into form now, moving it into the Law of Mind that is already making it so. Thank you, God for the wealth and abundance that is mine today and for the peace I now feel about it all. And so it is.

CARELL ZAEHN

MONEY

There is only One, One God, One Source, One Spirit, One Author and Creator of all. One Source of everything, One who creates all from nothing. One who always is present in me and in all. This is One, Mighty, Flowing All-Knowing, All-Powerful Kind, God.

This same One created me and loves me and cares for my good and is being me now. This One wants me to have faith always and has given me all I need already.

The Truth is that it has already been given. My goodness, my prosperity have already been created. My cash flow of $_____ a year from whatever source is already mine. I keep my eye on the promise of the Lord. I am as the lilies of the field. I give gracious thanks for my $_____ a year from whatever source, for all of my needs, wants and plenty to spare and share.

I express the gratitude I feel, knowing it is done. I am quiet and still and I am humble. I never lose faith that Holy Spirit in me, as my supply, is my supply. I am Self! I am worthy! I inherit the wealth of the Lord! I release the treatment. And so it is!

Nancy Callahan, R. Sc.P.

PERFECT ACCEPTANCE

There is only One—One Divine Source, One Infinite Presence and Power, One Ever-Present, Ever-Loving, Ever-Wise, fully Creative, unlimited Source of all Good that exists on this and all dimensions and at all moments.

Today and every day, I fully acknowledge and accept myself as a perfect, whole and complete individualized expression of this One, guiding, supportive and fully abundant Divine Source. I, too, am an ever-present and unlimited Source of infinite Power, Divine Love and Divine Wisdom.

As His perfect, unlimited, whole and complete expression of the Divine, I trust and accept that Spirit illumines and reveals everything I need to know in perfect and Divine Order; I trust and accept that it is safe for me to live courageously and to abandon all fear, as I am fully ever-supported by The One. I trust and accept that creativity easily and effortlessly expresses through me in perfect and Divine Order. I live in an abundant, perfectly-sourced, unlimited Universe. I know that my fullest acceptance of all of these Divine aspects of my being in no way takes away from or diminishes another. I trust and accept that my life unfolds perfectly in this and all moments and that all events transpire in a manner that assures both my highest and greatest good and the highest and greatest good of all concerned.

I live each and every moment of my life expecting and accepting perfect Divine Order in its greatest and most abundant sense. I now graciously accept that this Divine One is manifesting fully and perfectly, as me, in all aspects of my life and in the lives of others. I rejoice in each day that this One Source has made, and I give thanks for Its many blessings. I am so very grateful for this One Source made manifest and for this I give my sincerest thanks and greatest love.

And so it is.

CATHY COLE

EFFORTLESS COMPLETION

There is only One. This One is pure joy, pure love, and pure knowledge. This One is unlimited in all aspects and omnipresent on this and all dimensions. This One is an all-knowing, all-wise and all-loving Presence of pure and radiant light and It is unlimited creative energy. This One is perfectly whole, complete and truly all that is.

This One is now, at this very moment and at all moments, expressing as me. I am pure joy, pure love, pure knowledge and unlimited in all aspects. I, as this One, am also omnipresent in all dimensions and an all-knowing, all-wise, all-loving being of pure and radiant light and unlimited creative energy.

All I need to know is revealed to me calmly, serenely and peacefully. I now rest easily knowing that all my tasks are accomplished easily and effortlessly. There is plenty of time to accomplish all my responsibilities in a peaceful and orderly manner because I know that I of myself do nothing. During this time and at all times, I remember that I have a "senior Partner" who is there guaranteeing that all of my needs are met, including those pertaining to my work. Spirit is with me always and in all ways, assuring that my tasks are completed in perfect Divine Order. I now bless this overall process with love and know that the Universe has already provided all that I need to accomplish my tasks of the next week with ease, peace and integrity and for the highest good of all concerned.

I now let go and let God handle my next week of work and for this I am truly grateful. And so it is.

CATHY COLE

PERFECT TOOLS

Computers and cell phones, cars and refrigerators are not cause for aggravation in my life. Infinite Intelligence, the One Mind, is the first and only cause of my experience. This First Cause is the only cause in any of my affairs. That means that all my electronic and digital servants are at the command of this one Power. As odd as it may have seemed before, I now realize that when my copy machine isn't cooperating, I can remember the one First Cause. There's no need to kick the copier like it was a bad thing, or to curse my cell phone because it drops calls. I stop and take the time now to remember that God/Goddess/Spirit is present right here as my cell phone, as my car, as my computer. When these electronics are not functioning well, I honor the divinity within them and see them as a vehicle for Infinite Intelligence to operate in my world. I call upon that Infinite Intelligence to reveal Itself now, easily and effortlessly as I give great gratitude for the service of these pieces of equipment in my life.

I am willing to realize that if my cell phone is not operating, perhaps Divine Intelligence would rather have me be more attentive to something else. If the copier is malfunctioning, maybe I should slow down, take a God break and be less intense about my work. If my refrigerator is on the blink, I can ask where in my life am I on the blink as well. If my car isn't getting me to where I need to go, I can remember that God has no problem moving from one state of consciousness to another, so why should I.

My attitude about my appliances and electronic devices is now shifted from being something I am not to being the same as I – a configuration of the Divine Mind. From now on, I honor them that way.

With great thanks for the opportunity to remember who and what we all are, I release this treatment and it is done. And so it is.

CARELL ZAEHN

TAKING TESTS

A deep breath helps me get back to the center of pure being, back to Perfect Consciousness, Divine Intelligence that is omniscient, omnipresent and One with me now. There is only One Mind, God's mind, and because I am created in the image and likeness of God, I am made of the same God-stuff. That One Mind is my mind now. I am showing up for this test with the crystal clear awareness that the whole of Universal Mind, Perfect Reasoning and the light of Intuition are flowing through my mind. Universal Knowing has the right answer to every one of the questions, and I get my ego out of the way and let this divine infinite Intelligence in to answer the questions in the exact right manner, with all the right details. Every idea that the professor/director wants to read on my paper gets included in the perfect amount of detail.

Any doubts I had that I might not be smart enough, prepared enough, or anything enough are now eliminated as I let perfect Knowledge from the very First flow through me and take this test by means of me. My intuition is open and alert. My nervous system is at peace. I now see myself as already having aced this exam. This test is over; I did a great job, got a terrific grade, and I'm so pleased! I'm already experiencing the relief of knowing I did so well and that it's already all over with.

So, Law of Mind, here you go. Here's the directive. Make it a great exam! It's your job to go make it so. I'm just showing up at the exam room and you can do the work.

Great! I'm done with this. It's finished. Thank you, God for such a happy relief and for the great blessings that come to me for Your having done this through me. And so it is.

CARELL ZAEHN

JOY, BLISS AND HAPPINESS

The source of all joy is Shiva, God, the inner Self, the Self of all. This inner Self is bliss itself, the essence of joy, joy that requires no reason or excuse for being. Bliss and joy are my nature because I am the Self. I am not a person with a life, or a body, or a job. My identity is that I am One. As I am aligned with my true identity, the bliss and joy arise spontaneously, effortlessly and are steady.

I'm not taking my cause from others who have no sense of Self or even a limited sense of Self. Happiness occurs as I live my truth and remain inner-connected, in-dependent, in-comparable. Happiness is an inside job, and I rejoice that it is my birthright. I delight that not only is it mine to enjoy but that I have the opportunity to spread it around and share it with others. I allow my joy and happiness to light the way for others.

Regardless of life's circumstances, my inner truth remains the same: intact. My identity remains throughout all of life's changes. No matter what my karma brings around, I remember the Self that I am, and my joy is present through any difficulty, even the extreme moments. My happiness is not dependent on my circumstances because God is not dependent on circumstances. The inner Self is immutable, indestructible and eternal and so is my bliss.

That's the truth. The Law knows it. And so it is.

CARELL ZAEHN

Resources for Your Expansion

RELIGIOUS SCIENCE CHURCHES AND STUDY GROUPS
There are three branches of Religious Science:

United Church of Religious Science
Science of Mind Churches Worldwide
Science of Mind Magazine
www.religiousscience.org
www.scienceofmind.com
(818) 526-7757

Religious Science International
Creative Thought Magazine
www.rsintl.org
(509) 624-7000

Affiliated New Thought Network and The Emerson Institute
www.emersoninstitute.edu
www.newthought.org/members.html
(619) 640-0826

SIDDHA YOGA MEDITATION CENTERS WORLDWIDE
www.siddhayoga.org

Helpful Resources to Healing

Treatment is an astonishingly effective tool for removing blocks in consciousness and moving forward in your life. Sometimes our issues are buried. The source of the issues are often hidden from our conscious awareness and we are uncertain just how to address the problem. Although there are many good techniques and therapists to assist you in getting more clarity, I have two I would like to recommend. They both have the capacity to pinpoint the precise erroneous belief that is at the root of the issue. The techniques they use can clear the issue in one session, thus avoiding years of psychotherapy and enabling you to begin your treatment for eliminating the old pattern and installing a new one.

Dr. Rick Moss has developed Pre-Cognitive Re-Education, an extremely effective tool to target the subconscious pattern that needs to be identified, clearing the path so you can do specific treatment. This is a technique that frees the conscious and subconscious from negative and limiting beliefs and blockages, thus allowing one's innate and God-given perfection to be more fully expressed. That which we believe as well as the accumulated wounds of our personal history shape our present life experience. Pre-Cognitive Re-Education is a technique to help us, literally, change our minds and therefore our lives. It is an experience of performing "clearings" that address subconscious distortions and connect us with the power of Whole-Mind so we may release the negativity of the past, and realign with our magnificence. This work can be done by phone just as effectively as in person. Rick has an award - winning website for further information.

PRE-COGNITIVE RE-EDUCATION

DR. RICK MOSS. Ph.D.
P. O. Box 994
Carmel Valley, California 93924
www.essentialpathways.com
(831) 659-2313

The second modality is similar to the first in that it is also a kind of clearing. It is called Holographic Repatterning. In one 90-minute session, your practitioner will zero in on the event and the belief causing the problem. Once you know the event and belief, you can do your treatments to release it. This technique has many practitioners, and they too can work by phone as effectively as in person.

HOLOGRAPHIC REPATTERNING ASSOCIATION

P.O. Box 204
Glorieta, NM 87535
www.holographic.org

About the Author

DR. CARELL ZAEHN is a teacher of metaphysics, as well as a practitioner at the Pacific Coast Church of Religious Science in Pacific Grove, CA. She holds advanced degrees in Religious Studies as well as Education and French. For the past twenty-five years, she has immersed herself in spiritual practices that include both Eastern and Western teachings, meditation, and the healing arts that balance mind, body and spirit.

Carell's extraordinary skill lies in penetrating the surface of the issue and revealing what needs to be healed in consciousness in order to move forward. She has traveled across the country presenting lectures and seminars where her experience and resources are offered with great clarity, confidence, exuberance and delight. Carell stands for transformation and inner integrity through treatment, meditation and practical spirituality for the real world.

You may contact Dr. Carell for lectures, workshops, book signings and personal treatments at:

Dr. Carell Zaehn
Website: www.prayerthatworks.com
Email: zaehn2002@yahoo.com
Business phone (831) 626-0857
Toll-free (866) 481-5874

Please visit the website for:
>   Upcoming lectures and workshops
>   Treatment of the week
>   Monthly article of spiritual interest
>   Tapes of lectures and workshops

Appreciation to the following for their shared wisdom in this book

Phil Bertrand
MotivationMentor@aol.com

Dr. Ernest Holmes
The Science of Mind, 1998 ed. of the original 1926 text,
HI Productions, Encino, CA and *Words That Heal Today*

Carole King
words and music to *Beautiful*, copyright 1971, Colgems-EMI Music, Inc.

Dr. Bill Little
Pacific Coast Church, Pacific Grove, CA

Mary Manin Morrissey
author of *Building Your Field of Dreams* and *No Less Than Greatness*.
Living Enrichment Center, Wilsonville, OR

Thomas Troward
The Edinburgh Lectures, copyright 1904, DeVorss & Company, Camarillo, CA

Wayne Dyer

Marianne Williamson

Will Rogers

Mark Victor Hansen

Shakti Gawain

Nelly Wright

Eileen Caddy

Alan Cohen

C.S. Lewis

Ralph Waldo Emerson

Dr. Milton Erickson

P.D. Ouspensky and G.I. Gurdjieff

David Bohm

LaoTse

Jennifer Little

Gary Zukav

Notes and Reflections